THE VIOLENT
SOCIAL WORLD
OF BLACK MEN

THE VIOLENT
SOCIAL WORLD
OF BLACK MEN

William Oliver

LEXINGTON BOOKS
An Imprint of Macmillan, Inc.
NEW YORK

Maxwell Macmillan Canada
TORONTO

Maxwell Macmillan International
NEW YORK   OXFORD   SINGAPORE   SYDNEY

Library of Congress Cataloging-in-Publication Data

Oliver, William.
    The violent social world of black men / William Oliver.
      p. cm.
    Includes index.
    ISBN 0-669-27952-8
    1. Violence—United States. 2. Afro-American men. I. Title.
HN90.V5045 1994
303.6′0973—dc20   93-48216
                                                          CIP

Lexington Books
An Imprint of Macmillan, Inc.
866 Third Avenue, New York, N.Y. 10022

Maxwell Macmillan Canada, Inc.
1200 Eglinton Avenue East
Suite 200
Don Mills, Ontario M3C 3N1

Macmillan, Inc. is part of the Maxwell Communication Group of Companies.

Printed in the United States of America

printing number
1 2 3 4 5 6 7 8 9 10

For my Mother,
Alberta Freeman Baker:
You gave me life
and your love and wisdom
has meant so much to me.

For my Father,
Willie B. Oliver:
Your seriousness and
loyalty to family
have provided a good example
of how to live as a man.

W.O.

CONTENTS

ACKNOWLEDGMENTS

This book could not have been completed without the assistance of many people. First and foremost, I want to thank Dr. Hans Toch of the School of Criminal Justice, State University of New York at Albany and Chairman of my dissertation committee for his guidance, constructive criticism, editorial assistance, and most importantly, for believing in me during those times when I was ready to give up on myself. One could not have had a better dissertation committee than the scholars who collaboratively worked to shape my analysis of violence among black men. Thank you Drs. Graeme Newman, Robert Hardt, Richard Felson, and John Gibbs.

Dr. Frank Scarppitti, Chairman of the Sociology and Criminal Justice Department at the University of Delaware provided financial assistance, which allowed me to have the audio-taped interviews transcribed by Gail Brittingham, a master of the word processor with an ear for the slang spoken by black men.

Dr. Richard Majors, my friend and colleague, thank you for introducing me to Margaret Zusky, my editor at Lexington Books. I appreciate everything that Margaret and her staff, including Carol Mayhew and Tammy Fergus have done to transform a cumbersome research project into a reader-friendly book.

Finally, but not least by any means, I want to thank my daughter, Maya, for her love and support. Also, this book would not exist if the *"homeboys"* from my old *"hood"* didn't see the importance of sharing their personal experiences with me. Thanks fellas.

1

VIOLENCE AMONG BLACK MALES

T he United States has higher rates of violent crime than any other industrialized nation. Moreover, studies of the relationship between race and violent crime indicate that violent crime is primarily intraracial. For example, the FBI reports that in 1992, 94 percent of black murder victims and 83 percent of white murder victims were killed by members of their own race. Criminal victimization surveys have also documented the intraracial nature of interpersonal violence by analyzing the self-reports of assault, robbery, and rape victims.

Although blacks represent 12 percent of the general population, they are disproportionately represented among persons arrested for violent crimes. For example, in 1992 blacks represented 55 percent of the persons arrested for murder, 39 percent for aggravated assault, 34 percent for misdemeanor assault, and 61 percent for robbery. Moreover, blacks represented 50 percent of the 23,760 murder victims known to the police in 1990.[1]

No segment of the black community is immune to the personal and social devastation associated with black-on-black violence. All of the major sources of data on violent crime, however, consistently report that black violence is a social problem in which black males are most likely to be both the perpetrators and victims. The disproportionate representation of black males among perpetrators and victims of violent crime has been reported in arrest statistics, criminal victimization surveys, mortality reports, and numerous local studies of homicide and assault.[2]

Homicide rates among black men are generally six to seven times the

1

rates among white men. The U.S. Department of Health and Human Services reports that in 1990 black males had a homicide death rate of 68.7 per 100,000, compared with 8.9 per 100,000 for white males. Homicide is now the leading cause of death for black males 15–34 years of age. In 1987, homicide accounted for 42 percent of all deaths among young black males 15–24. Moreover, in 1990, black males in this age group had a homicide rate (138.3) more than nine times the homicide rate of young white males (15.4).[3]

In a recent study, the Bureau of Justice Statistics estimated that the lifetime risk of death by homicide is greater for blacks (1 in 21 for black males and 1 in 104 for black females) than it is for whites (1 in 131 for white males and 1 in 369 for white females).[4]

Consequences of Violence

In response to the prevalence of violence in their communities, many blacks manifest an overt fear of other blacks. According to Hannerz, "the people of the ghetto maintain a working knowledge of the potential for trouble in their environment."[5] Fear of blacks by blacks is typically expressed in terms of concern about avoiding trouble with others. In his article "American Tragedy: Blacks Killing Blacks," Sargent, a young black journalist, describes how blacks fear being victimized by other blacks when he asserts: "So when I am in poor black neighborhoods, I think about death and dying. It seems to be all around me and anxious to meet me. My heart goes out to young, impoverished, idle, hostile and ill-educated black men, but I try to keep a careful eye on them."[6]

Overt concern with avoiding trouble, particularly violent confrontations, has had an adverse impact on the lifestyles of lower- and middle-class blacks. Because blacks are aware that many males within the lower-class community adhere to values and norms that support the use of violence to resolve interpersonal conflict and as a means of obtaining money, many are becoming increasingly suspicious and fearful of their male neighbors. Hence, many blacks structure their daily activities to avoid dangerous people and places in order to reduce their risk of victimization. In this study of black males arrested for weapons-possession, Schultz found that many men justified carrying weapons by citing fear of being attacked with a weapon by other males in their neighborhood.[7]

Another way in which blacks cope with their fear of other blacks is to avoid social settings (like street corners, hangouts, bars, poolrooms, and parks) that are reputed to be dangerous places where violent confrontations and troublesome behavior are common. In independent studies of the social functions of black bars, for example, Sterne and Pittman, and Samuels have observed that low-income blacks are acutely sensitive to the risks involved in frequenting certain bars and street corners within the ghetto.[8]

The statistics reviewed above demonstrate that officially reported violence is disproportionately higher among black males than any other race-sex subgroup in America. Black-on-black violence is clearly a social problem of subs tantial human and practical importance.

Overview of Study

This study examines circumstances that lead to arguments and violent confrontations between black males while they frequent bars and bar settings such as after-hours joints, poolrooms, gambling parlors, greasy spoon restaurants, and street corners adjacent to bars.

The primary objective of the study was to concentrate on two aspects or processes of interpersonal violence: the behavioral sequencing of violent confrontations between black males in bars, and the intrapersonal definitions attached to situations that lead to violence in bars and the surface motivations of violent black men involved in such situations.

A major delimitation of the boundaries of this study is that it addresses only nonfatal interpersonal violence. While I have not excluded accounts of fatal violence, I was also interested in gathering data on nonfatal violence.

Much of what we currently know about violence and violent men is based on the analysis of arrest reports, medical examiner records, and interviews with institutionalized offenders. It has been estimated that for each single homicide committed, however, one hundred assaults are committed. Consequently, criminologists know very little about the sequence of events and the escalatory and de-escalatory processes associated with nonfatal violent confrontations. Moreover, extremely violent men—those who commit homicide—are atypical members of violent subcultures. According to Toch, "the more representative violence-norm carriers are lower-key aggressors, who we rarely meet in police lineups and crime statistics."[9]

Importance of the Study

The importance of this study is its potential contribution to symbolic interaction and subculture theories in uncovering how routine activities, definition of the situation, and interpersonal processes contribute to violent confrontations between black men.

Violent confrontations between black males also occur in a variety of other social settings, such as family residences, parks, schoolyards, shopping malls, and the like.[10] However, by opting to focus on violent confrontations that occur in bars and bar settings, I hope to enhance our understanding of how black men who frequent these settings define situations, what their cultural norms are, and the role that third parties play as factors contributing to the violent confrontations in which they are involved.

Most of the current research that examines interpersonal violence, moreover, focuses primarily on the sociodemographic characteristics of violent offenders and their victims, like sex, age, race, class; the temporal conditions associated with violent confrontations; and the alleged personality traits of violent offenders. According to Blumer, however, "neither of these two conventional approaches concerns itself first and foremost with the immediate violent act or with the experience of the violent offender and the formation and execution of his act."[11] Following the recommendations of Blumer and others, the present study uses the approach variously described as "process-oriented," "situation-centered," or "symbolic interactionist."

Finally, this study has practical implications, through its potential contribution to the design and implementation of violence-prevention programs. The findings from the study could be used, for example, to justify the establishment of violence-prevention programs that emphasize conflict-resolution or instituting alternative methods of socializing black males to assume masculine roles and lifestyles that reduce their potential involvement in violent confrontations.

Methodology

Forty-one black males were interviewed about their participation in violent confrontations that had occurred in bars and bar settings. In addition to having access to a sample of lower-class black males, this study was restricted to an examination of violent confrontations between black males because (1) black males have higher rates of violent crime offending and victimization than any other race-sex subgroup in America, (2) there are few studies that examine the intra- and interpersonal processes associated with violent confrontations between black men, (3) research on violence among blacks has failed to examine how predominantly black social settings (like bars and bar settings) affect the definition of interpersonal conflict or facilitate the sequence of events that leads to violent confrontations between black men, and (4) the findings from this research may enhance our understanding of the unique dynamics of black-on-black violence and provide data so that comparisons can be made between blacks and members of other racial and ethnic groups.

The interview schedule was designed to encourage these men to provide their unique perspectives on the intra- and interpersonal dynamics of the violent confrontations in which they participated.

Each respondent was asked to specify (1) the precipitating factor that led to the confrontation, (2) his feelings and attitudes as the confrontation unfolded, (3) the contribution of third parties, (4) his rationale for engaging in violent conduct, (5) whether he or his antagonist violated any social rules, (6) how alcohol or drug use contributed to the incident, (7) how the incident could have been prevented, and (8) the effect of the incident on his routine activities associated with frequenting bars and bar settings.

Limitations

I did not use systematic sampling procedures in this study because I was primarily concerned with interviewing black men who had previously participated in violent confrontations while frequenting bars or bar settings. Thus, a nonrandom snowball sample was obtained, consisting of men with whom I could make contact who were willing to participate in the research project. (Several potential respondents refused to participate in the study because I was unable to offer them monetary payment in return for interviews. If I had offered to pay respondents for their accounts, I could have increased the number of respondents interviewed and the number of incidents subjected to analysis.)

Because most of the incidents reported involved nonfatal assaults that were not reported to the police, external corroboration of the facts and events described by the respondents was generally not possible. However, I did not intend to use statistical analysis to reach my conclusions; rather, I was primarily concerned with uncovering data that would enhance my understanding of how social context, definition of the situation, and various situational factors converge and lead to violent confrontations between black men.

Definition of Terms

Violent Confrontation

In this study, the term *violent confrontation* is defined as an interpersonal transaction in which one or more individuals attempts to direct or actually directs physical force toward another person. Periodically, the term *violent incident* will be used as a synonym for *violent confrontation*.

Bars and Bar Settings

In this study, a distinction is made between bars and bar settings. *Bars* are defined as establishments licensed to sell liquor and beer to be drunk on the premises. Synonyms relevant to this definition include *taverns*, *nightclubs*, *lounges*, and *discos*.

The term *bar setting* is used to refer to the various after-hours joints, greasy spoon restaurants, poolrooms, gambling parlors, street corners, alleys, and parking lots that are generally located adjacent to licensed public bars.

Routine Activities

The term *routine activities* is used to refer to recurrent and prevalent activities in which individuals engage in order to provide for their basic needs, regardless of their biological or cultural origins: "Routine activities may occur at home, in jobs way from home, and in other activities away from home."[12]

Summary of the Remaining Chapters

Chapter 2 contains a review of selected literature and research related to major sociological theories that have been used to explain the disproportionate rates of violent behavior among black men.

Chapter 3 describes the social functions of bars in lower-class communities. Emphasis is placed on the use of bars as social stages to demonstrate adherence to the values, norms, and roles associated with compulsive masculinity.

Chapter 4 outlines the conceptual framework and lists the hypotheses that establish the boundaries of the research and the research rationale.

Chapter 5 describes the procedures and methods followed in conducting the study.

Chapter 6 reports findings related to hanging out as a major feature of the social world of lower-class black men.

Chapter 7 reports findings relevant to how black men justify their participation in violent confrontations in bars and bar settings.

Chapter 8 contains a general discussion of the findings, the hypotheses, and the prior research.

Chapter 9 consists of recommendations for additional research, public policy, and violence prevention.

2

PERSPECTIVES ON CAUSATION

To understand the factors that contribute to violence among black males, it is useful to review the literature that provides the theoretical and empirical context for its study.

Among students of violent crime, there is very little consensus on the causes of the high rates of violence among blacks. A number of explanations have been offered, including lack of impulse control, acquired biological causes (such as head injuries and the depletion of serotonin due to alcohol abuse), poverty, social disorganization and inadequate socialization, racial discrimination and displaced aggression, black self-hate, adherence to the norms of a subculture of violence, the cheapening of black life as a result of criminal justice leniency toward blacks who assault or murder other blacks, and self-destructive lifestyles centered on heavy drinking, drug abuse, drug-trafficking, and an exaggerated interest in material accumulation.[1]

Four Sociological Approaches to Black-on-Black Violence

This review considers four sociological theories—poverty–social disorganization, racial oppression–displaced aggression, subculture of violence, and contraculture—that social scientists have used to explain the high rates of criminal violence among black males. In addition, the compulsive masculinity concept is discussed.

7

The Poverty–Social Disorganization Theory

The poverty–social disorganization theory suggests that the disproportionate rates of criminal violence among blacks is a product of their high rates of poverty and a tendency to conform to lower-class cultural values and traditions.[2] Advocates of this approach are divided, however, with regard to whether it is poverty–social disorganization or deviant cultural traditions that are the primary factor contributing to the disproportionate rates of violence among blacks. Liberal scholars, for example, argue that poverty is a structural condition that leads to criminogenic social disorganization. More specifically, they have suggested that poverty contributes to the social conditions is typically associated with criminal violence, including chronic unemployment, teen pregnancy, female-headed families, academic failure, welfare dependency, inadequate socialization, and substance abuse.

In their classic longitudinal studies of juvenile delinquency among a birth cohort born in Philadelphia in 1945 (N = 10,000) and 1958 (N = 27,160), Wolfgang and colleagues found that low-income youth committed substantially more serious crimes and were more likely to become chronic offenders—five arrests or more before age 18—than youth from middle-income families. Their findings uncovered other indicators of an association between poverty and delinquency as well. They found, for example, that delinquency was also associated with residential instability and failure to graduate from high school.[3] Several other studies designed to examine the relationship between income level and homicide have found that poverty is positively associated with the ecological distribution of homicide throughout American society.[3]

Conservative criminologists and social scientists, for their part, have adopted a different perspective concerning the relationship between poverty, social disorganization, and criminal violence. They consider cultural values and traditions to be more significant than poverty in explaining violence among blacks. More specifically, they argue that the cultural values and traditions adopted by lower-class blacks lead to social disorganization and social conditions associated with criminal violence.[4]

Finally, in terms of the emphasis on generalized structural and cultural factors, both liberal and conservative scholars assume that poverty and social disorganization diminish the ability of the black community to encourage its youth to adopt conventional values and behavior.

The Racial Oppression–Displaced Aggression Theory

The racial oppression–displaced aggression theory of black-on-black violence is an extension of Merton's strain theory. Basically, strain theorists view deviance and crime as products of the anger and frustration experienced by people who are unable to achieve socially prescribed success goals.[5] The primary success goals that American society prescribes are academic achievement, occupational and social prestige, upward mobility, financial success, and material acquisition. To achieve these goals, individuals are encouraged to use legitimate means—that is, education, hard work, and goal-oriented activities that are legally permissible.

When access to legitimate means is blocked, however, some individuals adopt illegitimate means to achieve these same socially prescribed success goals. In addition, strain theorists argue that deviance and crime are more prevalent among members of the lower classes because they are more likely to have been denied equal access to educational and employment opportunities.

Expanding on the basic assumptions of strain theory, advocates of the racial oppression–displaced aggression theory believe that the disproportionate rates of violence among blacks is a by-product of racial oppression and economic exploitation.[6] Moreover, advocates of this perspective argue that racial oppression and economic exploitation are the primary causes of the social conditions—such as racial discrimination, academic failure, high rates of unemployment, poverty, and low self-esteem—that have induced "a chronic frustration situation" for many blacks.[7]

Advocates of this theory see two factors as primarily responsible for the "chronic frustration situation" that blacks experience. First, the majority of blacks support the basic values and goals of American society. Second, the American social system has been organized and structured to prevent the majority of blacks from achieving social, political, and economic equality with white Americans.[8] Consequently, advocates of this theory argue, high rates of violence among blacks are produced by the anger and frustration that blacks experience as a result of their inability to achieve socially prescribed success goals. Accordingly, advocates of this theory suggest, blacks are angry at white people and American society for subjecting them to a social status and social conditions that severely limit their ability to achieve the American Dream. Blacks are reluctant to direct their anger and frustration toward whites, however, out of fear of physical or economic retaliation. Thus, blacks are compelled to direct their anger and frustration inward or toward other blacks.[9] In sum, advocates of the racial oppression–displaced aggression theory have concluded, much of the violence among blacks is displaced aggression—that is, aggression directed toward the wrong source of frustration.

The Subculture of Violence Theory

The subculture of violence theory is one of the most popular and controversial explanations for criminal violence among blacks. According to Wolfgang and Ferracuti, the originators of this theory, the disproportionate rates of criminal violence among blacks are a product of their commitment to subcultural values and norms that condone violence as acceptable means of resolving interpersonal conflict. Pro-violence values and norms, they argue, are shared by all members of the subculture of violence. However, Wolfgang and Ferracuti also note that pro-violence values and norms are most prominent among males ranging from late adolescence to middle age.[10] Members of the subculture of violence develop favorable attitudes toward the use of violence through the processes of differential learning, association, and identification. Furthermore, many advocates of the subculture of violence theory believe, lower-class blacks are socialized in an environment in which the acceptability of violence as a means of resolving interpersonal conflict is culturally transmitted from generation to generation. Thus, most advocates of the subculture of violence theory have concluded that for members of the subculture of violence, nonviolence is a counternorm and that "violation of the expected and required violence is most likely to result in ostracism from the group."

The richest and most cogent description of subculture of violence values and norms has been provided by Miller in his classic article "Lower Class Culture as a Generating Milieu of Gang Delinquency." According to Miller, lower-class delinquents and criminals tend to adhere to focal concerns (that is, values and norms) that emphasize trouble, toughness, sexual conquest, manipulation, autonomy, and excitement. Although Miller is not primarily concerned with explaining interpersonal violence, advocates of the subculture of violence theory argue that the internalization of these values and norms and the subsequent definition of manhood in terms of these behavioral guidelines are a potent factor in the disproportionate rates of criminal violence among lower-class blacks.

The Contraculture Theory

Lynn Curtis is generally regarded as the originator of the contraculture theory of black-on-black violence. In its theoretical evolution, contraculture theory represents an extension of the subculture of violence theory. Its primary assumption is that "racial and economic constraints have causal primacy in determining black behavior but culture is a critical intervening variable."[12] Curtis argues that the disproportionate rates of criminal violence among blacks are primarily the result of cultural responses of a specific segment of the lower-class black male population to political, economic, and social conditions produced by institutionalized racial discrimination.

The violent contraculture is generally characterized by reference to its normative system—its set of values, norms, behavior, and traditions—to which a substantial number of lower-class black males adhere. A central feature of the violent contraculture normative system is the redefinition of manhood and the male role in a manner that exaggerates mainstream conceptualizations of manhood. Two factors, Curtis holds, have contributed to the persistence of the violent contracultural pattern of masculinity as a compelling alternative to traditional masculinity. First, institutional racism has prevented many lower-class black males from successfully enacting the male role as it is traditionally defined by the dominant culture.

Second, contraculture theorists argue, the persistence of compulsive masculinity and the violent contraculture are the result of male-to-male culture transmission of norms that emphasize toughness, sexual exploitation, manipulation, and thrill-seeking. Black males learn these norms and the behavior that they prescribe through processes of differential association, identification, and imitation.

Thus, advocates of the contraculture theory join subculture of violence theorists in arguing that the disproportionate rates of violence among blacks are a product of black males' adherence to a cultural code that condones violence-prone activities such as verbal challenges, sexual promiscuity, manipulating others, heavy drinking and drug abuse, gambling, and hanging out on street corners and in bars and other settings regarded as "dangerous places."[13] Derivatively, insults, threats to masculinity, and romantic jealousy become the primary factors contributing to violent confrontations between black males.

The Compulsive Masculinity Concept

Many social scientists have constructed theories of delinquency and violence that consider compulsive masculinity to be an important causal variable.[14] Most criminologists who have incorporated the concept in their theoretical discussions, however, have used it as an intervening variable rather than as an independent variable. Because the compulsive masculinity thesis is used frequently to explain the disproportionate rates of violence among black males, I shall formally discuss it below. Discussion of how it is used in criminological theories will be restricted to the poverty–social disorganization and racial oppression–displaced aggression theories. Its relevance to the subculture of violence theory was reviewed earlier.

Compulsive masculinity refers to a pattern of masculine behavior characterized by overt emphasis on norms of toughness, sexual conquest, manipulation, and thrill-seeking. Parsons introduced the compulsive masculinity concept in a paper that focused on the sources and patterns of aggression in the Western world.[15] He based his discussion of overt expressions of masculinity on the works of Freud and his followers, particularly in relation to what Freudians refer to as the "latency period," that is, a period during adolescence when boys feel compelled to repudiate identification with their mother in order to establish masculine identification.

According to Parsons, structural features of industrialized societies, especially the occupational system, create problems for boys in formulating a positive masculine identity. This problematic masculine identification, he argued, arises as a result of boys' greater association and identification with their mothers, due to the conspicuous absence of their fathers from the home and from involvement in childrearing. As boys approach and enter adolescence, their identification with their mothers become exceedingly problematic, because during this stage they experience intense social pressure and anxiety precipitated by fear that their male peers will perceive them as physically or emotionally weak. Hence, many boys adopt sentiments antithetical to characteristics associated with femininity. In this context, masculinity is defined in terms of toughness, emotional detachment, independence, sexual conquest, and competitiveness.

Following Parsons's lead, many social scientists have studied the manner in which compulsive masculinity is expressed.[16] Although these writers differ with respect to terminology—employing terms such as *compulsive masculinity, overt masculinity, exaggerated masculinity, conspicuous masculinity,* and *macho*—the patterns of behavior they describe are indistinguishable.

A major area of debate and disagreement among students of compulsive masculinity is the origins and maintenance of compulsive masculinity. Parsons argued that compulsive masculinity is not a functionally dominant pattern of the adult masculine role but a momentary reaction formation that typically occurs during a male's transition from boyhood to manhood and in his subsequent participation in the occupational system. Implicit in Parsons's conceptualization of compulsive masculinity is the assumption that its expression is for most boys a temporary state, typically diminishing in significance as they move into the occupational system.

Parsons's conceptualization of the origin of compulsive masculinity is based on a structural perspective. In the decades since Parsons, students of compulsive masculinity who adopt the structural perspective have tended to play down the rejection of mother-emphasis that Parsons offered and instead emphasize the impact of structurally induced economic marginality in explaining why individuals adopt the compulsive masculinity alternative. Toby, for example, argues that adherence to compulsive masculinity ideals is more prevalent among lower-class males due to their inability to wield symbolic power—influence and prestige derived from family background, educational achievement, income, social and political connections, and material acquisitions.[17]

On the other side of this debate are those who see the origins and maintenance of compulsive masculinity as cultural rather than structural. Advocates of this cultural perspective argue that males who adopt the compulsive masculinity alternative do so as a consequence of their socialization into a cultural milieu that encourages males to adopt norms of toughness, emotional detachment, sexual conquest, manipulation, and thrill-seeking.[18] A major assumption of the cultural perspective is that compulsive masculinity is the result of a cultural outlook and lifestyle that is radically present-oriented and that attaches no value to work, sacrifice, self-improvement, or service to family, friends, or community. Thus, Miller asserts that compulsive masculinity involves a "positive effort to achieve states, conditions, or qualities valued within the actors' most significant cultural milieu."[19] In sum, advocates of the cultural perspective argue that social disorganization and cultural traditions are the primary factors contributing to the origins and maintenance of compulsive masculinity.

Black Males and the Compulsive Masculinity Alternative

In his ethnographic study of lower-class blacks residing in Washington, D.C., Hannerz characterized compulsive masculinity as an alternative to traditional masculinity. The traditional masculine role prescribes that men be self-sustaining, achieve success within the occupational system, and protect and provide for their families. Two factors have contributed to the origin and persistence of compulsive masculinity as a compelling substitute norm for the traditional masculine role. First, lower-class black males can adopt the compulsive masculinity alternative to mitigate the low self-esteem and negative feelings that emerge as a consequence of their inability to enact the traditional masculine role. Second, the persistence of the compulsive masculinity alternative among many lower-class black males is a product of male-to-male cultural transmission of norms emphasizing toughness, sexual conquest, manipulation, and thrill-seeking. These men learn these norms and the behavior they prescribe through the processes of differential association, identification, and imitation.[20] In sum, reason Hannerz and others, many lower-class black males have adopted the compulsive masculinity alternative due to their vulnerability to systematic deprivation of equal education and employment opportunities and their attraction to the coping style and compensatory strategies of a particular group of black males within their immediate cultural milieu.

A Dysfunctional Compensatory Adaptation

The term *compulsive masculinity alternative* describes a compensatory adaptation that many lower-class black males adopt to cover up their inability to meet the standards of the traditional masculine role. According to Staples:

> Since other symbols of masculinity have been denied to many black males, the status conferral system in black life attributes high levels of esteem to those males able to demonstrate their proficiency in fighting and sexual exploitation of black women.

But instead of being an effective strategy to cope with environmental stress such as racial discrimination, economic exclusion, and low self-esteem, the compulsive masculinity alternative is a dysfunctional compensatory adaptation. Rather than solving problems in the environment, it generates additional ones.[21] Black males' adherence to the sexual conquest norm, for example, is a major factor contributing to the high rates of teenage pregnancy (25 percent), children born out of wedlock (55 percent), divorce (220 per 100,000), and female-headed families (50 percent) among blacks.[22]

Compulsive Masculinity and Violence

Several major criminological theories have either implied or explicitly held that compulsive masculinity is a major factor contributing to the high rates of violence among blacks. Black males' adherence to compulsive masculinity, for example, is explicitly included in the poverty–social disorganization theory of black-on-black violence. Frazier, Miller, and Moynihan maintain that the cultural values and norms of lower-class black males are responsible for the high rates of crime among blacks.[23] Moreover, advocates of this perspective argue, the high rates of violence among black males is the result of their inadequate socialization and the failure of ghetto institutions to encourage lower-class black boys to value conventional definitions of manhood.

Advocates of the racial oppression–displaced aggression theory of black-on-black violence refer to compulsive masculinity as a compensatory adaptation or style that black males adopt in order to cope with structural pressures that prevent them from enacting the traditional male role. Moreover, advocates of this perspective argue, the dominant social structure encourages black males' adherence to compulsive masculinity through its tolerance of those black men who commit violent acts against other blacks. For example, after observing the operation of the southern criminal justice system, Dollard concluded: "It is clear that this differential application of the law amounts to a condoning of Negro violence and gives immunity to Negroes to commit small or large crimes so long as they are on Negroes."[24]

Advocates of the subculture of violence theory have been most prone to embrace the compulsive masculinity thesis as an important causal variable associated with the high rates of interpersonal violence among blacks. In a frequently quoted statement regarding how compulsive masculinity contributes to homicide, Wolfgang states:

> Quick resort to physical combat as a measure of daring, courage, or defense of status appears to be a cultural expectation, especially for lower socio-economic class males of both races. When such a culture norm response is elicited from an individual engaged in social interplay with others who harbor the same response mechanism, physical assaults, altercations, and violent domestic quarrels that result in homicide are likely to be relatively common.[25]

Critics of the compulsive masculinity thesis tend to use the same arguments against it that are used to question the validity of the subcultural violence theory. Erlanger and Ball-Roheach, for example, on the basis of independent research designed to determine whether members of the lower class subscribe to values distinct from those held by middle-class, have concluded that members of the lower class do not maintain distinct values that condone violent conduct.[26] In a recent study, Brownfield attempted to test the Moynihan version of the compulsive masculinity thesis by analyzing self-report data in which 1,500 white males and 1,000 black males were administered a questionnaire on their family background and personal involvement in criminal behavior.[27]

According to Moynihan, the disproportionate number of female-headed families among blacks is causally related to crime and delinquency. Brownfield found that contrary to the compulsive masculinity perspective advanced by Moynihan, the physical absence of the father is unrelated to the self-reported violent behavior of black and white boys. In addition, Brownfield found, black and white boys whose fathers have a history of unemployment are more likely to engage in violent behavior than are sons of fully employed fathers. Although Brownfield's findings refute Moynihan's version of the compulsive masculinity perspective, his data do not invalidate versions of the thesis that consider compulsive masculinity to be an adaptation to structural pressures.

Alcohol and Violence

Criminologists and other social scientists have long considered alcohol to be a significant risk factor associated with assault and homicide. The presence of alcohol in homicide has primarily been determined through medical examiner records and arrest reports.

In this classic study of homicide in Philadelphia, Wolfgang found that 53 percent of the 588 homicide victims killed between 1948 and 1952 had been drinking prior to their victimization, and that in nearly 44 percent of the homicides, both victim and offender had been drinking.[28] Wolfgang also found that prehomicide alcohol use was higher among male victims (56 percent) than female victims (42 percent). He also observed significant racial variations in prehomicide drinking among homicide victims. For example, he found that 70 percent of black male victims, compared with 50 percent of white male victims, had been drinking prior to their victimization.

In a more recent study of alcohol use and homicide, Goodman and colleagues conducted an analysis of medical examiner records of 4,092 homicide victims who were killed between 1970 and 1979 in Los Angeles.[29] Although a total of 4,950 individuals were killed during this period, only 4,092 of the victims were tested for prehomicide alcohol consumption. Goodman and colleagues found that 46 percent of the victims had been drinking prior to their victimization. Male homicide victims (51 percent) were almost twice as likely to have been drinking than female homicide victims (26 percent). Like Wolfgang, Goodman and colleagues found racial variations in prehomicide alcohol consumption. For example, they found that Hispanic victims (57 percent) had the highest rates, followed by blacks (48 percent) and whites (38 percent).

Goodman and colleagues' research has confirmed previous research findings that alcohol-related homicides tend to occur on weekend days more often than on weekdays and that alcohol use is greater among persons killed in bars or restaurants (75 percent) than in other types of settings (39 percent).

The presence of alcohol is also associated with the victim-offender relationship. For example, Wolfgang found, victims who had been drinking (74 percent) were more likely to precipitate their death than victims who had not been drinking (60 percent).

Although Goodman and colleagues did not examine the association between alcohol consumption and victim-precipitated homicide, they did examine prehomicide alcohol consumption and type of homicide incident. Consequently, they found, victims killed during physical fights motivated by an argument between the combatants (53 percent) were more likely to have been drinking than victims (20 percent) who were killed in a crime-related situation such as robbery, burglary, or rape. Hence, their findings suggest, primary homicides (homicides that primarily involve relatives and acquaintances) are more likely to be associated with prehomicide drinking than are secondary homicides (homicides in which the participants are primarily strangers).

Studies of assault have also identified alcohol as a significant situational factor leading to its occurrence.[30] In their study of arrest reports of 25 percent of the 965 aggravated assaults that occurred in St. Louis in 1961, for example, Pittman and Handy found that 25 percent of the victims and offenders had been drinking prior to the assault.

The presence of alcohol in homicide and assault has also been examined in self-report surveys administered to incarcerated offenders. According to a Bureau of Justice Statistics report published in 1983, 84 percent of the prisoners incarcerated for murder reported that they drank lightly to heavily (41 percent) or very heavily (43 percent) prior to committing the offense for which they were currently incarcerated. Eighty-six percent of the prisoners incarcerated for assault reported that they drank lightly to heavily (41 percent) or very heavily (45 percent) prior to committing their current offense.

Drugs and Violence

Criminologists and other social scientists have only recently begun to examine the relationship between drugs and violent crime. In a study designed to assess the relationship between drug use and homicide, Zahn and Snodgrass have found that drug users have higher rates of homicide than nondrug users.[31] Moreover, in an earlier study, Zahn and Bencivengo found that young black male drug users had a higher risk than members of all other race-sex subgroups for being victims of drug-related homicides.[32]

In a recent study of homicide in New York City, Tardiff and colleagues found that 30 percent of the male and 20 percent of the female homicide victims killed in 1981 had one or more drugs in their body at the time of their death. Morphine and other opiates were the most common types of drugs, found in 11 percent of the victims. Cocaine was found in 3 percent of the victims.[33]

In a recent survey of inmates in state correctional facilities, the Bureau of Justice Statistics found that 33 percent of the prisoners incarcerated for violent offenses reported that they had been under the influence of a drug prior to committing their current offense.[34] More specifically, they found the following pre-incident drug-use patterns for prisoners incarcerated in 1986: robbery (42 percent), kidnapping (37 percent), assault (29 percent), murder (28 percent), sexual assault (25 percent), and manslaughter (20 percent). These data suggest that a significant proportion of the prisoners who were using drugs prior to committing their current offenses were convicted of violent crimes (robbery) or property crimes (burglary) associated with monetary gain.

Goldstein has developed an explanatory typology to categorize various types of drug-related violence. In his typology he describes three types of drug-related violence: psychopharmacological, economic compulsive, and systemic.[35]

The term *psychopharmacological violence* is used to describe violent incidents precipitated by the ingestion of drugs and their subsequent psychological and/or pharmacological effects. These effects may include drug-induced excitability, paranoia, irrational thought, or aggressiveness.

Economic compulsive violence refers to violent incidents in which an individual is motivated by a desire to obtain money to purchase drugs. Robbery is the most common type of economic compulsive violence.

Goldstein's third category of drug-related violence, *systemic violence*, refers to violent incidents involving disputes associated with drug-trafficking. Systemic violence involves turf disputes, robbery of drug dealers, and violent acts committed against drug users by drug dealers for nonpayment or other issues related to drug-trafficking.

Conclusion

Theories of violent crime causation tend to reflect either a structural or cultural emphasis. Subsequently, however, these perspectives tell us very little about how structural and cultural factors converge to influence the evolution of values, norms, roles, and lifestyles that increase the likelihood of violence participation. In the following chapter, I describe the cultural significance and social functions of black bars and street corner settings. An important aspect of this study is the examination of violent confrontations that occur in public social settings—bars and street corners—where black males tend to congregate for a variety of reasons.

3

BLACK BARS: SOCIAL FUNCTIONS AND COMPULSIVE MASCULINITY DISPLAYS

A ttempts to live up to the normative ideals of compulsive masculinity have a substantial effect on the routine activities and lifestyles of black males prone to become involved in violent confrontations. As a result of the adverse impact of structural constraints, black males have less access to socially approved masculinity-conforming settings than white males. Consequently, bars and bar settings have evolved into one of the most significant social settings in the black community with respect to masculine role socialization and the enactment of compulsive masculinity role orientations.

A major shortcoming of the compulsive masculinity literature is that much of it gives the impression that adherence to compulsive masculinity values and norms automatically translates into overt actions and that men who adhere to compulsive masculinity norms are constantly fighting, exploiting women, drinking, and gambling. I believe, however, that commitment to compulsive masculinity is symbolically displayed more than it is enacted through violence. Moreover, these displays mostly occur in certain norm-structured social settings and situations. Implicit in this assertion is the belief that individuals who repetitively demonstrate or overtly act out their commitment to compulsive masculinity role orientations risk being socially ostracized, physically victimized, and/or imprisoned. Consequently, many lower-class black males rely on symbolic displays in order to communicate their commitment to compulsive masculinity.

The term *symbolic display* is used here to refer to the use of verbal and nonverbal cues to signify an individual's commitment to a particular ideal, value, norm, or role. While symbolic displays are the primary means that lower-class black males use to demonstrate their commitment to compulsive masculinity, however, they may also serve as a catalyst for violent confrontations between black males. Therefore, I will provide an overview of how black males use bars and bar settings as social stages to demonstrate their commitment to values and norms associated with compulsive masculinity.

Bars and Bar Studies

Among the various social institutions that exist in American society, few have been more seriously neglected by social scientists than the public bar. A standard definition of a bar is "an establishment licensed to sell liquor and beer to be drunk on the premises."[1] Bars are also referred to as taverns, grills, clubs, and discos. While this definition is accurate, it fails to convey the cultural and institutional significance of bars in our society.

Those studies of bars that have been conducted vary with respect to methodology and range of analysis, but the role of bars as important social institutions is acknowledged across the board. The fact that bars function in our society as "primary meeting places where social relationships with other persons can be established" elevates bars to the status of valued social institutions.[2] According to Macrory, the cultural and institutional significance of bars is in facilitating social integration, especially for urban dwellers who seek a sense of belonging, recognition, and security.[3]

The Social Functions of the Lower-Class Black Bar

In her ethnographic study of bars that are generally patronized by whites, Cavan characterizes bars as "unserious social settings." Moreover, she argues that the behavior in which bar patrons engage has no consequences for them in their lives outside bar settings. She describes barroom behavior as a form of play and time out from real life, "when the constraint and respect the social world ordinarily requires is no longer demanded."[4]

Implicit in Cavan's characterization of bars as "unserious social settings" is the assumption that the typical white bar patron possesses a personal biography that encompasses one or more serious and socially respected roles. Thus, white bar patrons who engage in outrageous or deviant behavior in bars are generally shielded from negative labeling as a result of their successful participation in serious social settings like school, family life, the workplace, and civic organizations.

Contrary to Cavan's observations, however, ethnographic studies suggest that unlike white bars, black bars tend to be regarded as serious social settings, and that behavior engaged in while frequenting black bars often has personal and social consequences for black bar patrons in their lives outside the bar setting.[5] The importance of black bars is primarily due to the fact that many black communities substantially lack social institutions that offer blacks the opportunity to socialize and engage in status-enhancement activities.

Thus, a major aspect of the lower-class black bar's cultural and institutional significance is its role in providing many lower-class blacks with an opportunity to engage in roles and social activities that certain segments of the black community highly value. Many lower-class black males use bars and bar settings to exhibit their ability to dress and dance well, to attract the attention of members of the opposite sex, to control and manipulate the behavior of others, and to demonstrate their knowledge of controversial issues and worldly activities such as male-female relationships, childrearing, race relations, politics, sports, gambling, alcohol, and drugs. Thus, because of the significant link between successful bar participation and enhanced social status and self-esteem, the bar is located at the center of lower-class black social life.

The cultural and institutional significance of the lower-class black bar is also evidenced by the varied manner in which blacks utilize this social setting. One of the most important functions of the black bar, for example, is its use as the primary setting where lower-class blacks can initiate and develop heterosexual relationships. There is no other institution or social setting within the black community that is so closely identified with the establishment and maintenance of heterosexual relationships.[6]

Another major social function of the lower-class black bar is its use as a black-oriented social setting where blacks may go in order to interact and socialize with other blacks. Black bars allow lower-class blacks the opportunity to escape personal and social stressors that they frequently confront as result of racial discrimination, unemployment, poverty, family instability, lack of achievement, and low self-esteem. By participating in various bar activities like drinking, conversing, dancing, listening to music, and pursuing members of the opposite sex, many lower-class black bar patrons attempt to purge themselves of the anxiety and frustration associated with their experience of being black and lower class in America. Thus, the ultimate social function of the black bar is its use as a supportive social setting in which blacks may engage in socially approved cathartic releases such as conversing in black dialect, singing, dancing, consuming alcohol and drugs, engaging in other expressive actions designed to relieve themselves of tension and anxiety.

In addition to these major social functions, lower-class black bars are also places where messages may be left and received, where information regarding the availability of drugs or stolen merchandise may be sought, where inexpensive space may be rented for wedding receptions, birthday parties, and club meetings, where people may seek shelter from inclement weather, and where people may go in order to escape the demands of family life and the boredom of daily routine.

Given the diversity of social activities and functions associated with the lower-class black bar, many students of black social life have concluded that the bar is one of the most important institutions in the black community. According to Lewis and Samuels, the black bar is in many ways equal to the black church in terms of the pronounced role it plays in the social organization of the black community. Moreover, Lewis and Samuels have concluded on the basis of their independent research findings that the lower-class black bar has a significant impact on the self-concept, behavior, and lifestyle of a large segment of the lower-class black community.[7] Although the black bar setting provides lower-class blacks with an opportunity to engage in time-out activities, participating in these activities does not occur without reputational implications.

As a departure from Cavan's characterization of bars as unserious social settings, I am suggesting that lower-class blacks perceive the bars that they frequent as both unserious and serious social settings. The unserious dimension is the frequenting of bars to engage in time-out activities, including socializing with friends, drinking, dancing, and interacting with members of the opposite sex. However, because they are aware of the reputational implications that their peers attach to how they engage in time-out activities, lower-class blacks are sensitive to the fact that frequenting black bars and bar settings may lead others in the setting to evaluate their conduct either positively or negatively relative to subculturally relevant normative standards.

My analysis in this regard is consistent with the views of Goffman, who argues, "The cultural values of an establishment will determine in detail how the participants are to feel about many matters and at the same time establish a framework of appearances that must be maintained, whether or not there is feeling behind the appearances."[8]

Masculine Expression in the Black Bar

Black males frequently use black bars as social stages in which they act out rituals associated with compulsive masculinity. Symbolic displays of compulsive masculinity are, of course, expressed in other social settings like barbershops, poolrooms, gambling parlors, and street-corner hangouts. Because of the absence or relative absence of women in these other settings, however, symbolic displays designed to signify one's adherence to compulsive masculinity are less credible than are symbolic displays expressed within heterogeneous bar settings.

During adolescence, many lower-class black boys learn that an important step toward social recognition and acceptance as a man is developing the ability to successfully interact in bars and bar settings. Prior to actually going to a bar, many lower-class black boys have been told about or have overheard conversations pertaining to bars and the activities that occur within them. Relatives and older friends are a major source of this information and cultural socialization.

The importance of the bar and the activities that occur within it are also communicated to lower-class black boys when they witness the "going out" preparation rituals in which adult relatives and friends engage prior to venturing out for a night on the town. Prior to "going out," for example, many lower-class black males spend an inordinate amount of time coordinating their clothing, cultivating their physical appearance, and mentally going over the way they will enact their self-presentation. Consequently, because of the relationship between bar patronage and sex role socialization, heterosexual interaction, and enhancement of social status and self-esteem, frequenting bars is akin to a manhood rite of passage for many lower-class black males. Engaging in symbolic displays of compulsive masculinity while frequenting bars is a commonly accepted means of projecting and reinforcing the masculine self-image and social identity.

The Toughness Norm and the "Tough Guy" Image

A central feature of lower class black males' definition of masculinity is the belief that toughness—physical prowess, emotional detachment, and willingness to resort to violence to resolve interpersonal conflict—is an omnipresent characteristic of masculinity. These men symbolically display their adherence to toughness as a norm by appearing and remaining cool in social situations perceived as potentially threatening to their self-image or physical safety. Because the lower-class black bar is recognized as a high-risk social setting, offering the likelihood of threats to self-image and/or physical safety, symbolic displays designed to communicate an individual's toughness is an essential component of impression management and masculine self-presentation within this setting.

Coolness is the primary medium by which black men symbolically communicate their adherence to the "tough guy" image. According to Lyman and Scott, "Coolness is defined as poise under pressure. . . . [It] refers to the capacity to execute physical acts, including conversation, in a concerted, smooth, self-controlled fashion in risky situations, or to maintain affective detachment during the course of encounter involving considerable emotions."[9] According to Folb, the term *cool* "connotes a variety of things depending on context."[10] For example, coolness can be a strategy utilized to "make yourself interesting and attractive to others so that you are better able to manipulate their behavior along lines that will provide some immediate gratification."[11] To be cool, in terms of presenting oneself as tough, requires that males structure their behavior to give the impression that they are independent, always in control, and emotionally detached. Thus, demeanor, style of walking and physical posturing, and "tough talk" are major strategies that lower-class black males employ to symbolically communicate their adherence to the toughness norm.

Demeanor. In his study of the presentation of self in everyday life, Goffman found that interpersonal interactions are facilitated by individual "performances." According to Goffman, "performances refer to all the activity of an individual which occurs during a period marked by his continuous presence before a particular set of observers and has some influence on the observers."[12] In this sense, symbolic displays designed to communicate adherence to compulsive masculinity norms are a form of impression management.

A significant feature of the symbolic display of toughness is demeanor. The primary function of demeanor is to assist a man in creating an image of himself for the purpose of communicating to those in his immediate presence that he has certain desirable or undesirable qualities. Deportment, dress, and bearing constitute the major elements of demeanor.

With respect to demeanor and masculine presentations of toughness within the lower-class black bar, lower-class black males often attempt to present themselves as unapproachable and tough. By adopting a "cool front," with facial gestures, poise, and a calculated aloofness, these men symbolically communicate their adherence to the toughness norm, or what Majors and Mancini Billson describe as a "cool pose."[13]

Style of Walking and Physical Posturing. Style of walking and physical posturing are other strategies that lower-class black males utilize to communicate their adherence to the toughness norm and the "tough guy" image. Studies of nonverbal communication among lower-class blacks indicate that blacks attach a great deal of significance to stance, physical posturing, and style of walking. According to Cooke, most blacks, particularly black males, can alternate their walks depending on what the situation calls for.[14] Both Suttles and Cooke agree that stance, physical posturing, and style of walking constitute a significant set of communicative devices for blacks.[15] Through assessment of an individual's stance, physical posturing, and style of walking, other bar patrons are able to glean information regarding an individual's values and behavioral propensities. The convergent displays of stance, physical posturing, and style of walking are employed to communicate the impression of being fearless and willing to resort to violence as a means of resolving interpersonal conflicts.

"Tough Talk." Black culture is often referred to as an oral culture, due to the unique emphasis blacks place on verbal skill and storytelling. Research in black sociolinguistics suggests that blacks are very sensitive to the power of words to comfort, to wound, to sexually arouse, and to enhance social status.[16] Within black bars and bar settings, for example, it is not uncommon for lower-class black males to engage in "tough talk." A common theme of "tough talk" stories is the storyteller's successful management of a conflict-ridden situation. The storyteller highlights the seriousness of the situation by his description of how he successfully managed a potential threat to his self-image and/or physical safety.

The complex nature of communicating one's adherence to the "tough guy" image and toughness norms through "tough talk" is reflected in a man's personal account of what he said to an antagonist, or how he manipulated his demeanor, or how he used verbal threats or violence to manage a situation that he perceived as potentially threatening to his self-image, reputation, or physical safety. "Tough talk" stories tend to involve conflicts within a wide range of interpersonal relationships, including those with friends, acquaintances, strangers, girlfriends, wives, social workers, police, and others who might challenge a man's manhood or autonomy.

Because many lower-class black males lack the resources of education, adequate employment, income, and material acquisitions that are necessary to enact the traditional masculine role, a significant number of them have opted for an alternative definition of masculinity. The "tough guy," the "player of women," the "thrill-seeker," and the "hustler" are the most common alternative manhood role-orientations that lower-class black males adopt. These roles are primarily oriented toward the support of norms that encourage violence, the emotional and economic exploitation of females, and chronic participation in high-risk activities such as hanging out on street corners and in bars, heavy consumption of alcohol and drugs, gambling, and petty crime. Moreover, these roles are often adopted as a means to facilitate status-enhancement.

Due to the fact that a significant number of lower-class black males lack the symbols typically associated with traditional masculinity and respectability, there is intense status competition among these males to establish identity in terms of the compulsive masculinity alternative. Consequently, identity challenges are a significant feature of social interaction among lower-class black males. In independent studies, Suttles, Hannerz, Samuels, and Anderson have found that challenges of an individual's account of his commitment to norms related to toughness, sexual conquest, or thrill-seeking were frequently the cause of heated character contests.[17] On most occasions, these contests are regarded as an entertaining feature of social interaction. However, all of these researchers noted that identity challenges sometimes lead to violent confrontations.

Generally, when a lower-class black male is confronted with an identity challenge, he will attempt to mitigate the impact of the challenge by ridiculing or "sounding" on the transgressor. If such a strategy fails to deter the antagonist, however, or fails to appropriately repair the damage done to his identity or reputation, the man may employ violent means. Students of black sociolinguistics report that blacks refer to the nonviolent aspect of this pattern of identity defense and identify promotion as "woofing." Cooke describes woofing as "a style of bragging and boasting about how bad one is." Kochman argues that the purpose of woofing "is to gain without actually having to become violent, the respect and fear from others that is often won through physical combat. To accomplish this, it is necessary for a man to create an image of being fearless and tough, someone not to be trifled with." Woofing is primarily a symbolic act in that it is a form of talk designed to advertise one's willingness to engage in violence.[18]

Generally, an individual engaging in woofing does not want the confrontation to escalate into violence. Due to the intense competition for status among lower-class black males, however, and their awareness that many of their peers use talk as a means of enhancing their social status, identity challenges and woofing are frequently employed to check an individual's masculinity credentials. Thus, identity challenges and woofing are often critical situational factors that influence the interpersonal dynamics of violent confrontations between lower-class black males, especially in bars and bar settings.

The importance of symbolic displays of toughness is not limited to the defense or promotion of identity. But because of their intense competition for status, lower-class black males quickly learn that accurately evaluating the behavioral cues and symbolic displays of other males is helpful in determining what other men value and what type of behavior to expect from them. A man who is interested in sizing up another man's commitment to the "tough guy" image, for example, will pay close attention to the other man's demeanor, physical posturing, style of walking, and "tough talk" and how he handles himself when talking to women, gambling, or drinking.

Furthermore, how others evaluate a man's symbolic displays will affect his role and status within street-corner and bar settings. These evaluations will determine the degree of deference that others show him as well as the degree of deference he is expected to show to those who outrank him. Assessments of an individual's symbolic displays of toughness, however, are not regarded as reliable indicators of that individual's commitment to violence or his proficiency in managing actual violent confrontations. This is because lower-class black males are acutely aware of the performance aspects of promoting oneself as a "tough guy." Therefore, the most reliable measure of a man's commitment to toughness is personally witnessing him in action or hearing about his prowess against a bona-fide opponent from a reliable informant.

Black males who are unable or unwilling to engage in symbolic displays of toughness are often labeled "weak" or "chumps." Such labeling has the additional consequence of restricting the defamed individual from participating as an equal in the primary peer groups that hang out at various bars. Negative labeling may also increase a man's vulnerability to being victimized by men who are interested in promoting or enhancing their identity as con men or "tough guys" at the expense of a weaker person.

The Sexual Conquest Norm and the "Player of Women" Image

Among the various functions of the lower-class black bar, none is more important than that of facilitating the initiation and development of heterosexual relationships. Because many lower-class black males tend to define masculinity in terms of dominance and the sexual exploitation of women, the "player of women" image is the primary medium through which they symbolically display their adherence to the sexual conquest norm. The "player of women" image is a symbolic display characterized by efforts to attract more than one woman, maintain exclusive sexual access to most of the women with whom one is involved, and exercise control over a woman's emotions and economic resources.

Within bars and bar settings, black males symbolically display adherence to the sexual conquest norm more often than any of the other compulsive masculinity norms. This is largely due to the fact that adherence to the sexual conquest norm encompasses a wide array of symbolic displays that frequently overlap with overt demonstrations of female exploitation. Moreover, many lower-class black males go out of their way to avoid trouble, especially interpersonal conflict likely to require overt demonstrations of toughness. Symbolic displays of adherence to the sexual conquest norm and the player of women image are also very common because they promote a sense of camaraderie among lower-class black males, whereas symbolic displays and overt demonstrations of toughness are more likely to generate tension and conflict among them. The extent to which a man adheres to the sexual conquest norm is typically assessed in terms of the number of women he is observed with in various social settings (including the bar), the physical attractiveness of the women he is involved with, and his ability to demonstrate control over a woman's behavior and economic resources.

Black males engage in a series of symbolic displays (like personal dress and grooming, peer group announcements, raps and semiprivate conversations, socializing with women, and escorting women to and from bars) in order to communicate to other males their proficiency in manipulating and "playing" women.

Personal Dress and Grooming. Several studies of lower-class blacks have found that black males attach a great deal of importance to clothing and style of dress.[19] Moreover, these studies suggest that lower-class black males often utilize clothing as a symbol to communicate individuality, values, and behavioral propensities.

In his comparative study of clothing purchases of black and white males,

Schwartz found that black men were prone to purchase clothing based on style and the advertised social advantages to be derived from owning a particular garment. White men, on the other hand, were found to more often purchase clothing based on comfort and fit. Thus, Schwartz concluded, black men are more likely to utilize clothing to promote their self-worth than are white men.

In order to facilitate heterosexual interactions in bars and bar settings, lower-class black males tend to adopt a specific set of personal dress and grooming patterns. Within the lower-class black community there is no other social setting, with the exception of the black church, that generates such an intense concern with dress and grooming as does the black bar. Prior to frequenting a bar, particularly on nights or occasions when a significant number of women are known or expected to be present, many black males will spend a great deal of time and energy coordinating their clothing and styling their hair in order to effect a socially attractive public presentation. In her study of urban black teenagers, Folb observed that for lower-class black males, "Being well dressed is not only a way of upstaging others but of demanding attention and, therefore, space. So the more conspicuous the display, the more expensive the outfit, the more ammunition you have to game on others."[20]

Grooming is another important feature of lower-class black males' masculinity displays. The popularity of various hairstyles is always in a state of flux. However, grooming itself is less significant than the communications embedded in personal dress. Heterosexual interactions within lower-class black bars and bar settings are substantially affected by a man's personal dress. Through assessment of a man's personal appearance, a woman who is interested may glean significant information regarding his values, self-concept, degree of adherence to the various compulsive masculinity norms, and access to financial resources. Most black women are very adept at distinguishing hustlers and pimps from those black males who are not as intensely committed to the overt expression of compulsive masculinity. Developing the ability to assess men based on their personal dress and public presentation is a skill that many black women develop in order to protect themselves from men who are committed to the exploitation of women. Although black women generally reject the idea of establishing relationships with males who adhere to the more overt aspects of compulsive masculinity, Hannerz has observed that some black women are attracted to the flashy self-presentation that successful pimps and hustlers project. Hence, black women are not entirely adverse to getting involved with men who adhere to the more overt aspects of compulsive masculinity. Consequently, because they are aware that many black women are attracted to the flash of the pimp and the hustler, many lower-class black males incorporate elements of the pimp style in their self-presentations, especially when frequenting bars and other settings where women are present.[21]

Style of Walking. In his study of nonverbal communication among blacks, Cooke found that black males engage in three styles of walking. These include the basic soul walk, the cool walk, and the pimp walk. Despite the differences among them, Cooke asserts that "the function of the walk remains the same: to attract attention and admiration, especially from females."[22]

Regardless of the style of walking that a black male adopts, he will demonstrate it on occasions when he frequents bars and bar settings. Personal dress, grooming, and style of walking often converge to constitute an important catalyst in facilitating heterosexual interactions between black men and women.

In discussing the symbolic display of toughness, respondents mentioned style of walking as an element of male-directed coolness—coolness designed to communicate a man's commitment to the toughness norm and the "tough guy" image. With respect to the sexual conquest norm and the "player of women" image, style of walking is designed to attract the attention of females. In this case, style of walking is an element of female-directed coolness—coolness designed to communicate to women that one is stylish, contemporary, worldly, romantic, and adept at fulfilling women's needs. Other elements of female-directed coolness include personal dress, grooming, raps, and semiprivate conversations.

Peer Group Announcements. A substantial portion of male peer group conversation and repartee in black bars revolves around peer group announcements of an individuals' adherence to the sexual conquest norm—that is, dominance and control over women by means of emotional manipulation and the active pursuit of female sexual partners. Typically, such repartee escalates as peers challenge the claims of one of their members, questioning the accuracy of a man's announcements pertaining to emotional detachment from and/or sexual success with a particular woman. Generally, conversation and repartee related to sexual conquest and control over women is conducted in a conspiratorial tone, especially if women are within hearing range. Making peer group announcements regarding one's orientation toward women is similar to "tough talk," except that peer group announcements are designed to communicate a man's adherence to the sexual conquest norm and the "player of women" image. Occasionally, peer challenges of an individual's peer group announcement lead to strained relationships and interpersonal conflicts. On most occasions, however, peer group announcements pertaining to one's adherence to the "player of women" image and peer challenges of such announcements constitute a form of verbal entertainment and cultural sharing within black bars and bar settings. "Thus claiming and debunking become important ingredients in the ghetto-specific mode of interaction between peers, and loud verbal contests are a recumbent part of those social occasions during which the men regard themselves as 'having a good time'."[23]

Among the symbolic displays that these black men employ to communicate adherence to the sexual conquest norm and the player of women image, peer group announcements are salient in most discussions of females. In his research, Samuels found, "Public confessions in incontinence are routine. The men take pride in having themselves confirmed in the status of 'stud,' or an exploiter of women who can 'love them and leave them.' To perform in private without an accompanying public disclosure is to miss out on a crucial dimension of an affair."[24]

Raps and Semiprivate Conversations. The most common manner of initiating heterosexual relationships in lower-class black bars is by male-initiated "raps and semiprivate conversations." "Rapping, while used synonymously to mean ordinary conversation, is distinctively a fluent and lively way of talking which is always characterized by a high degree of personal style. Rapping is employed at the beginning of a heterosexual encounter to create a favorable impression and to be persuasive at the same time. Consequently, men rap to women in the hope of getting sex."[25]

Because of the importance of the lower-class bar as a meeting place for men and women, black men expect each other to actively pursue women in this setting. To be overheard or seen rapping to a woman communicates to other men (both primary and secondary peers) a man's adherence to the sexual conquest norm and the "player of women" image. Blacks often define the symbolism of male-female interaction, especially in bar settings, as leading toward a sexual relationship.

Generally, the first line of a rap is a compliment. If the woman being approached appears responsive, the rapping proceeds in an undertone, as the rapper seeks to make a favorable impression on the woman. He also wants to create the impression of intimacy between himself and the woman to whom he is directing his rap. Another goal of the rapper is to obtain as much information as possible on the woman's availability. Thus, the rapper attempts to determine whether the woman is escorted by a man, where she resides and with whom, whether she has a job, and whether she is currently involved in a close emotional relationship with a man. If the rapper is able to obtain this information, he will then decide whether it is worth it to escalate his pursuit of the woman.

In most male-female encounters the woman being rapped to has the right to terminate the inquiries and interaction at any time. A common termination technique that many black women employ involves telling the rapper that she is involved with a man. This technique is used by women who actually have an ongoing relationship with a man as well as by those who do not. This technique is often employed during the early stages of the male-female encounter. Other termination techniques may include nonverbal putdowns, ignoring compliments, and forceful verbal insult.[26]

Regardless of what transpires in male-female encounters, both parties are aware that such interactions are open to public scrutiny. Hence, heterosexual relations are initiated publicly, but in a semiprivate context. The public nature and enclosed space limitations of bars render interpersonal interactions between patrons visible to interested and noninterested others. Black men and women are also willing to engage in semiprivate conversations, moreover, because of the social rewards (like enhanced self-esteem and social status, respect, and admiration) that can result from being seen rapping or interacting with an attentive and attractive person of the opposite sex. Consequently, the social status of a lower-class black male is enhanced if he is perceived as able to successfully initiate intimate relationships with women.

Because a man's rapping to a woman is generally conducted in an undertone, his progress with her is determined by observing the woman's facial gestures and body language. A man is perceived as making progress with a woman if her facial gestures suggest, for example, that she is enjoying the compliments and attention being paid her. On the other hand, if the woman being rapped to is not smiling and if her responses appear to be caustic, the man is perceived as not making any progress. If a man appears to be making no progress with a woman, however, he will not lose face among his primary peers and other males if he has a bona-fide record of success with other women.

Some additional indicators of making progress with a woman include being allowed to purchase a drink for her, dancing with her (especially slow dancing), being allowed to monopolize the time she spends in the bar, and escorting her home. Escorting home a woman whom one has just recently met is highly regarded. Often such an action becomes the subject of a peer group announcement at some later converging of the peer group.

To confirm their peer group announcements of sexual conquest and substantiate their verbal claims, lower-class black males will sometimes deliberately initiate public displays with their new conquest. A man might escort a woman out for a night on the town for the sole purpose of symbolically communicating to other males (both primary and secondary male peers) his sexual access to her and his emerging control over her emotions and economic resources. Other social settings such as house parties, dances, concerts, and recreational events may also be scenes of symbolic displays designed to communicate sexual conquest.

In situations where a man has not announced a sexual conquest, his primary peers will allow him a substantial amount of time to consummate the relationship, as long as he has an ongoing relationship where sexual conquest and dominance have been confirmed. Men who do not have such a relationship to point to and who have failed at initiating a heterosexual relationship as a result of their rap are likely to be subjected to ridicule and negative labeling.

Bar-Hopping. Another symbolic display that black men employ to communicate their adherence to the sexual conquest norm and the "player of women" image is bar-hopping. Typically, bar-hopping involves making periodic stops at several bars in the course of a limited time span. A common bar-hopping pattern in which lower-class black males engage occurs on Friday and Saturday nights—the two nights when black bars are most likely to be patronized by a substantial number of women. Usually on these nights black men will travel back and forth between the various bars within the network of bars they frequent. The primary goal of bar-hopping is to locate "the action"; in this case the action is the bar that is most festive and offers the greatest opportunity for initiating a new heterosexual relationship. As they travel from bar to bar, these men attempt to rap to different women within each establishment. Once the bar rounds are completed, these men generally return to the bar in which a particular woman was the most responsive or interesting, out of the various women they approached while bar-hopping.

Men who have developed ongoing relationships with two or more women also engage in bar-hopping. By bar-hopping, these men attempt to maintain and nurture their relationships by being out with the various women with whom they are involved on the same night, but in different bars and bar settings.

More often than not, bar-hopping is a peer group activity involving two or more individuals. The act of traveling back and forth between bars with the intent of initiating heterosexual relationships or maintaining already sexually consummated relationships with women reinforces the "player of women" image and symbolically communicates adherence to the sexual conquest norm. It is not uncommon for lower-class black males to make peer announcements regarding their commitment to the sexual conquest norm and the "player of women" image while traveling to and from various bars. In these instances peer announcements constitute a form of self-promotion, social integration, and entertainment.

The Manipulation Norm

Many studies of lower-class black culture have suggested that black males attach a great deal of importance to the ability to outwit, manipulate, and control others through the use of their wits. Moreover, studies of black sociolinguistics indicate that lower-class black males employ language for a variety of purposes having to do with fulfilling the normative requirements of the compulsive masculinity alternative. For example, they use language to ward off punishments or retribution, to promote their self-image, to enhance their status at the expense of others, to manipulate and control people and situations, and to entertain.

Tall Stories. During the course of social interaction within bar settings, lower-class black males symbolically display their adherence to the manipulation norm by telling tall stories. Tall stories often feature the storyteller as protagonist and focus on his successful nonviolent management of a conflict-ridden situation, in which the circumstances, if he had not controlled them, could have resulted in a serious threat to his self-image and/or physical safety. Generally these stories center on crises having to do with appropriate adherence to the toughness and sexual conquest norms.

Men symbolically display their adherence to the manipulation norm within the context of verbal contests and peer challenges of peer group announcements. Hannerz found that "a good verbal style in encounters is recognized as a useful tool in the business of life, and those men who are known as skilled manipulators of interpersonal transactions gain some prestige from it among their peers."[27]

In most symbolic displays in which a lower-class black male tells tall stories while frequenting a bar, his primary goal is to communicate to others the keenness of his wit and his ability to outsmart others. Peer challenges to the verbal claims of others are often initiated by a man who seeks to enhance his social status by making the other person appear to be less committed to compulsive masculinity norms than he has claimed to be. However, Hannerz has also noted that not "all prestige is accrued from being a good talker have to do with the strictly utilitarian aspect. A man with good stories well told and with a quick repartee in arguments is certain to be appreciated for his entertainment value."[28] Thus, it is through tall stories and peer group announcements that the norms indicative of compulsive masculinity are culturally transmitted among lower-class black males. The good talker and storyteller is admired and respected because he is a major transmitter of the compulsive masculinity tradition.

The Autonomy Norm

Autonomy from external control has been a major concern of black males, dating back to the American slavery era.[29] *Autonomy* here refers to an individual's concern with being free from external control in the conduct of his or her personal life. In describing the autonomy concerns of lower-class black males, Miller asserts that "on the overt level there is a strong and frequently expressed resentment of the idea of external controls, restrictions on behavior, and unjust or coercive authority."[30] Consequently, symbolic displays designed to communicate a man's adherence to the "tough guy" or "player of women" image are ultimately assertions of his personal autonomy. In many of their interpersonal conflicts, black males often express intense concern about asserting personal autonomy. Coolness and verbal announcements are the primary means that lower-class black males utilize to symbolically display their adherence to the autonomy norm.

Coolness. Presenting oneself as cool—that is, publicly projecting emotional self-control and aloofness—is one way in which lower-class black males symbolically demonstrate their adherence to the autonomy norm in bars and bar settings. Their symbolic displays may include facial gestures, body language, and nonchalant verbal responses.

Verbal Announcements. Symbolic displays of autonomy may also take the form of verbal announcements in which individuals assert their adherence to the autonomy norm. For example, within lower-class black bars it is not uncommon to overhear someone assert: "I'm my own man" or "I do what I want to do" or "I do my own thinking." Men often make these assertions in response to peer challenges of their autonomy claims, particularly their assertions of independence and dominance in heterosexual relationships. Another context in which men make verbal announcements is during accounts of their behavior in conflict-ridden situations involving potential threats to their self-image and/or physical safety.

Conclusion

This review of the social functions of bars and bar settings strongly suggests that black males attach a great deal of importance to how they behave and are perceived by others when frequenting these settings. It appears that bars and bar settings are used as social stages where lower-class black men construct and enact socially approved masculine identities and therefore achieve a sense of significance.

In the following chapter, the conceptual framework for the questions I asked of the black men I interviewed regarding their participation in violent confrontations is discussed.

4

TOWARD THE DEVELOPMENT OF A CONCEPTUAL FRAMEWORK

There are very few studies that specifically examine barroom violence. Graham and colleagues conducted an observational study of violent incidents in 185 bars in Vancouver, Canada; a major finding they reported is that the distribution of aggression in bars is not random.[1] A factor analysis of 160 incidents of physical aggression and 113 incidents of verbal aggression indicated that barroom violence occurred most often in bars with the following characteristics:

Unclean and inexpensive surroundings

An atmosphere of suspiciousness and hostility

Unfriendly bar workers

Few limits on acceptable behavior

A large number of unemployed patrons or patrons involved in illegal work such as prostitution and drug dealing

A majority of patrons who are members of minority groups (American Indians, blacks, and homosexuals)

Patrons who spend an inordinate amount of time at the bar and use it as a home base for other activities

Heavy drinking

35

Campbell and Marsh[3] have also examined barroom violence. In their study, they analyzed 2,000 questionnaires completed by owners of White-bread pubs in the United Kingdom. Approximately 35 percent of the respondents reported one or more fights involving men in their pubs within a two-year period. They also noted that the age of the bar owners and location of pubs were associated with barroom violence.

Other studies have also noted that age is an important predictor of barroom violence.[4] In a study of bars in Vancouver, Canada, Graham and Trumbull found that violent confrontations were most likely to occur in bars that catered to young patrons. Bars that serve youthful patrons are more likely than those that serve older patrons to become settings for incidents of verbal and physical aggression and verbal incidents that escalate into violent confrontations. Felson and Steadman report that "one of the reasons why aggression occurs in bars is that they are places where young adults congregate and come into contact."[5]

The predominance of males among persons involved in barroom brawls has been consistently reported in contemporary studies of barroom violence. According to Marsh, "Some pubs are always going to have the odd fight within them because they are traditional settings in which to settle scores, demonstrate macho qualities or engage in other ritual ceremonies."[6]

Social class has been associated with barroom violence. For example, Felson and colleagues found that bars with a lower-class clientele are more likely to experience incidents of verbal aggression than bars patronized by middle-class clients. They also found that neighborhood bars were more likely to experience incidents of physical violence than bars that draw clients from a wider geographical area.[7]

Contemporary studies of barroom violence, however, have largely failed to specify what factors precipitate the sequence of events leading to violent confrontations in bars. This lacuna in the literature is primarily due to the fact that most studies of barroom violence have been based on interviews of bar owners and bartenders. These studies do, however, provide some insight into the interpersonal dynamics of barroom violence. For example, Felson and colleagues interviewed bar owners and bartenders in 131 bars in Albany, New York, and 67 bars in Ireland. With respect to factors that cause barroom brawls, they found that the refusal to serve a patron was a major factor contributing to conflict between bar workers and patrons.

Felson and colleagues also found that there was a much greater frequency of aggression and violence in American bars than in Irish bars. However, "fights in American and Irish bars generally occur over similar issues."[8]

In his study of violence in English pubs, based on interviews of bar owners and bartenders, Marsh concluded that barroom violence is often precipitated when some men deliberately use the bar setting to enhance their status by retaliating against people who they believe have cast aspersions on their honor or reputation.[9] Finally, Curtis found that bars, poolrooms, street-corner hangouts, and family residences were the primary settings in which violent confrontations occurred between lower-class blacks. This observation, as well as prior research on barroom violence, suggests that the black bar would make an excellent research site to study interpersonal violence among blacks. At this time, however, no one has conducted research that specifically examines the interpersonal processes associated with violent confrontations in black bars. References to violent confrontations in bars and bar settings have been noted in several participant observation studies of black communities.[10]

Three Theoretical Traditions

The research questions and hypotheses that I have sought to answer and test in this study have evolved from the conceptual integration of three distinct theoretical traditions, including: the structural-cultural approach, the routine activities approach, and symbolic interactionism.

The Structural-Cultural Approach

The most fundamental assumption of the *structural-cultural approach* is that the disproportionate rates of criminal violence among blacks is a product of structural pressures and dysfunctional cultural adaptations to those pressures.[11] More specifically, historical and contemporary social practices involving institutional racism—that is, the systematic deprivation of equal access to opportunity—have prevented a substantial number of black males from achieving manhood through legitimate means. Thus, a considerable number of black males in each succeeding generation adopt alternative means of expressing masculinity.

The term *compulsive masculinity alternative* has been used by Hannerz to refer to an alternative style of masculine expressiveness that many lower-class black males adopt (see Chapter 3). Black males who adhere to the compulsive masculinity alternative define manhood in terms of overt toughness, sexual conquest, manipulation, and thrill-seeking. As we have seen, the values and norms that constitute the ideological foundation of the compulsive masculinity alternative have contributed to the emergence of two major black masculinity role orientations: the "tough guy" image and the "player of women" image.

The "tough guy" image is a masculinity role-orientation based on a set of norms that define manhood in terms of fearlessness, emotional control, and a willingness to use violence to resolve interpersonal conflict. The "player of women" image is a masculinity role-orientation based on a set of norms that define manhood in terms of overt promiscuity, dominance, and emotional and sexual exploitation of women.

Given the pronounced effect that the "tough guy" image and the "player of women" image have on the behavior of black men and on interpersonal relations among blacks, it is inevitable that these exploitative and unreciprocal role-orientations would produce a unique set of motives and justifications for assault and homicide among black males.

Routine Activities Approach

The second theoretical perspective underlying this study is the *routine activities approach*. Advocates of this approach argue, based on independent analyses of victimization data, "that lifestyle differences are associated with differences in exposure to situations that have a high victimization risk. According to Hindelang and colleagues, individual lifestyle patterns evolve from specific sets of routine daily activities, both vocational activities (work, school, keeping house) and leisure activities. Cohen and Felson have defined *routine activities* as "any recurrent and prevalent activities which provide for basic population and individual needs, whatever their biological or social origins." Thus, routine activities may occur at home, in jobs away from home, and in other activities away from home.[11]

Hindelang and colleagues have also stated that an individual's specific routine activities are influenced by role expectations and structural constraints that establish social boundaries that either expand or constrain behavioral and lifestyle options.

Role expectations are defined as "cultural norms that are associated with achieved and ascribed statuses of individuals and that define preferred and anticipated behavior."[12] Because role expectations vary as a function of age, for example, children under 12 years old consistently have low rates of criminal victimization. This finding reflects the fact that the routine activities of children under 12 tend to take place in highly supervised social settings like home and school. Moreover, there are no social expectations that children under 12 should work outside the home or frequent public places at night. Both of these situations have been found to increase the risk of victimization.

Structural constraints are defined by Hindelang and colleagues as "limitations on behavioral options that result from the particular arrangements existing within various institutional orders, such as economic, familial, educational and legal order."[13] For example, a lack of economic resources increases the likelihood that an individual will reside in a neighborhood near a disproportionate number of individuals who manifest offender characteristics. Thus, individuals who have access to sufficient funds can reduce their risk of criminal victimization.

Advocates of the routine activities approach have primarily focused on describing how role expectations and structural constraints converge to produce sets of routine activities that either increase or decrease the risk of criminal victimization. In addition, they have described how "the spatiotemporal organization of social activities help people translate their criminal inclinations into action."[14]

Cohen and Felson have suggested that in order for an offender to commit a direct-contact predatory violation like assault or homicide, the routine activities of victim and offender must independently unite them in space and time. Subsequent to their meeting in space and time, three factors must exist before a direct-contact predatory crime can occur. The factors they list include a motivated offender, a suitable target, and the absence of capable guardians against a violation. Furthermore, they argue that the absence of "any one of these elements is sufficient to prevent the successful completion of a direct-contact predatory crime."[15]

In sum, the routine activities approach argues that an individual's lifestyle influences the opportunity to engage in criminal behavior and also increases or decreases the risk of criminal victimization.

While the routine activities approach was not initially constructed to specifically explain the disproportionate rates of criminal victimization among blacks, a fundamental assumption of the perspective is that race is a powerful social demographic characteristic as a result of its malleability to structural constraints and role expectations. For example, victimization data consistently report that blacks have higher rates of criminal victimization than whites or Hispanics. In addition, black males have higher rates of victimization than any other race-sex subgroup.

Unemployment and low income status are major structural constraints affecting the routine activities of black males. A recent study of unemployment among black males found that nearly half (46 percent) of the nine million working-age black males between the ages of 16 and 60 were unemployed in 1983.[16] Moreover, labor force participation rates of black males 20 to 24 have decreased dramatically since 1960. In 1960, for example, 82 percent of black males 20 to 24 participated in the labor force, but in 1980 only 73.5 percent of this group participated.[17]

The high rates of academic failure and unemployment among black males increase the likelihood that their routine activities will limit their ability to isolate themselves from persons who possess offender characteristics. This point is consistently supported by victimization data. For example, black males have higher rates of criminal victimization than any other race-sex subgroup. In addition, academic failure and unemployment contribute to the inordinate amount of time black males spend frequenting bars, street corners, and other public places at night.

Symbolic Interactionism

The third theoretical approach underlying this study is *symbolic interactionism*. The most fundamental assumption of symbolic interactionism is that behavior that occurs within an interpersonal context is generally a product of interpretation and definition of the situation.[18]

The meaning of a situation is interpreted through a two-phase process. Phase one involves *definition of the situation*. During the definition of the situation phase the individual looks at what is happening and indicates to himself what is happening and/or what is likely to happen in the situation.[19]

Phase two of interpretation involves *judgment*. Here, the individual decides how he should act in the situation, given his definition of it. The judgment phase is substantially influenced by the individual's interpretation of how some specific "generalized other" views him and the situation that he confronts. Thus, definition of the situation leads to a consideration of the perspectives of a "generalized other" and his interpretation of the "other's" perspective on a given situation that he draws on in situations that he confronts.

While symbolic interactionists typically define *generalized other* as an abstraction that operates as an alter ego and not as a set of specific norms and values, they do not reject the importance of culture in influencing definitions of the situation. For example, Stokes and Hewitt have suggested that definition and reaction to problematic situations occur in a situational context in which "participants in interaction interpret one another's acts within a cultural framework."[20]

Summary of Integrated Theoretical Perspective

The integration of the structural-cultural approach, the routine activities approach, and symbolic interactionism allows for the construction of a theoretical framework that describes how macrosociological factors (like social structure, racial discrimination, and poverty) and microsociological factors (like role-orientations, values and norms, routine activities, and definitions of the situation) converge and produce disproportionate rates of interpersonal violence among black males.

The integrated theoretical perspective consists of a three-stage macro-microsociological process. First, historical and contemporary patterns of racial discrimination against blacks have forced a substantial number of black males to adopt masculine role-orientations that encourage commitment to values and norms that emphasize toughness, sexual conquest, manipulation, and thrill-seeking.

Second, structural constraints (like lack of access to adequate educational opportunities, chronic unemployment, and low-income status) and compulsive masculinity role-orientations lead many black males to engage in routine activities (like spending an inordinate amount of time frequenting bars and bar settings, and participating in activities associated with the use and sale of drugs) that increase the risk of becoming involved in violent confrontations.

Finally, structural constraints, compulsive masculinity role-orientations, and the routine activities associated with the enactment of those role-orientations are responsible for the emergence of a criminogenic social context that increases black males' risk of violence participation. These conditions, however, are not independent causes of violence. Ultimately, the sequence of events leading to violent confrontations among black males is precipitated by how they define themselves, their antagonists, and the problematic situations in which they find themselves.

Hypotheses

Given the assumptions of the integrated theoretical perspective, the data that I have collected will be analyzed to test the validity of the hypotheses listed below.

1. Violent confrontations between black males while frequenting bars and bar settings are generally precipitated by one or both combatants interpreting the other as engaging in rule-violating behavior associated with the expression of compulsive masculinity.
2. The occurrence of interpersonal conflict between black males while frequenting bars and bar settings often leads to face-saving concerns and actions due to the presence of third parties.
3. Given the public visibility of violent confrontations that occur in bars and bar settings, third parties often influence the outcome of these encounters.
4. Involvement in a violent confrontation in a bar or bar setting leads many black males to alter routine activities associated with frequenting bars and bar settings.

Conclusion

The conceptual framework of this study did not allow me to test the validity of culture norm-centered theories, nor to find evidence that permitted me to endorse one version of the perspective over others. What I did do, however, was to frame questions that allowed violent black men to discuss subculturally relevant assumptions, such as those described in the compulsive masculinity, subculture of violence, and contracultural perspectives. Should individuals who have been involved in violent confrontations, particularly black men in conflicts with other black men, spontaneously bring up such assumptions in response to open-ended questions, this would add plausibility and provide documentation to premises that those cultural theories hold in common.

In the next chapter, the methods and research sample of the study will be outlined.

5

METHODS AND SAMPLE

T his study is primarily concerned with uncovering how violent black men define and account for their involvement in violent confrontations occurring in bars and bar settings. In order to fully inventory the factors that lead to violent confrontations as perceived by the participants, the research method and design follows prescriptions implied in the phenomenological and symbolic interaction perspectives.

Phenomenologists and symbolic interactionists believe that the most effective method of gaining insight into a particular social phenomenon is to analyze the personal accounts of individuals who have been involved in it. The phenomenological perspective directs the researcher to examine the feelings, motives, thoughts, and perceptions behind people's actions. Moreover, the phenomenological approach examines reconstruction of the event being examined in terms of what happened and why it happened.[1]

The phenomenological research strategy has been used to examine a broad range of topics in the fields of criminology and criminal justice, including the accounts of prisoners incarcerated for committing violent offenses;[2] the lifestyles and attitudes of hustlers;[3] factors contributing to prison-induced mental health crises among prisoners;[4] prison sexual violence;[5] the lifestyles and concerns of prisoners on death row;[6] domestic violence;[7] and the excuses and justifications of rapists.[8]

Interview Procedures

In this study the focused interview was used to gather data related to how forty-one black males define and account for their involvement in violent confrontations. The focused interview was adopted primarily because it was originally designed to tap the subjective perceptions of individuals who have participated in a particular experience.[9] This data-gathering technique is also useful because it places respondents in a role that approximates that of co-researchers into their personal experiences, thus providing a motivation for participation and introspection.

All of the interviews were recorded with a portable tape recorder. The interviews were open-ended; however, the interview schedules were designed to tap specific topics. The specific questions subsumed under each of the topical headings are detailed in full below, in the Appendix of this study.

Sample Size and Selection

This study was conducted in a city in upstate New York. Preliminary observations of this community indicated that there were six predominantly black public bars, three predominantly black after-hours joints, and two greasy spoon restaurants.

Incidents that occurred in the two after-hours joints and the two greasy spoon restaurants are included in this study because these unlicensed bar settings represent an integral feature of the local social scene. These settings facilitated many of the same activities that occurred in the licensed public bars. Music, dancing, and alcohol, for example, are available at the after-hours joints and the greasy spoon restaurants. The special function of the after-hours joints and the greasy spoon restaurants is to provide bar services during hours in which bars are required by law to be closed. That is, these settings provide music, dancing, alcohol, and a setting to engage in social interaction almost twenty-four hours a day. Moreover, these settings provide opportunities to engage in illegal gambling, drug-dealing, drug use, and other types of criminal activity.

Studies of urban lifestyles have referred to the network aspects of bars, after-hours joints, poolrooms, greasy spoon restaurants, barbershops, and their adjacent street corners, alleys, and parking lots as gathering places that together function to facilitate sociability.[10]

In the principle sample, forty-one black males known to have been involved in a violent confrontation in a bar or bar setting in the last six years were interviewed.

During the summer of 1983, I indicated to several bar owners, bartenders, and bar patrons that I was interested in interviewing them about factors associated with arguments and fights in black bars. Thus, prior to conducting the interviews, I had established contact with several informants who indicated a willingness to assist me by sitting for interviews as well as referring me to other persons who had been involved in a violent confrontation in a bar or bar setting. Though the sample is an opportunity sample, this networking procedure maximized the probability of securing experienced respondents and of enhancing rapport with them.

Process

Prior to conducting the interviews on violent confrontations between fall 1987 and summer 1988, I had spent approximately four years (from 1983 to 1987) frequenting six predominantly black public bars, two after-hours joints, and three greasy spoon restaurants that were routinely patronized by lower-class black males residing in this upstate New York community. These bars and bar settings were regarded as the most dangerous in the city by local residents, police, and criminal prosecutors.[11]

The first stage of this study involved the initiation of a participant observation field strategy in order to systematically examine the social functions of the black bar and how black males interacted with each other and with females in this setting. The purpose for engaging in participant observation was twofold. First, I wanted to be certain that I understood the cultural context in which violent confrontations occurred between black males in bars and bar settings. Second, by deliberately placing myself in the role of a fellow patron, I would be able to make contact with individuals who might be willing to undergo intensive interviewing regarding their involvement in a violent confrontation.

During the participant observation stage, I frequented the bars and bar settings on weekdays, weekends, at all hours of the day and night, and during every season of the year. Due to the fact that I was either a full-time graduate student or employed ninety miles away from the research site, however, a disproportionate portion of the observational data was gathered during weekends, holidays, and the summer months.

My own role among the men I observed and those I subsequently interviewed changed over time. I would characterize my role as both an insider and outsider in this setting, or an "insider without." As the research progressed from participant observation (summer 1983 to summer 1987) to participant observation plus actively seeking respondents to provide personal accounts of violent confrontations (between summer 1987 and summer 1988), my role as an insider without became very clearly defined to me and those with whom I had contact.

My insider status derived from the fact that I was a "homeboy" with solid credentials. That is, I had grown up in the area, and many of the bar and bar setting regulars, aged 28 to 45, knew me as a former member of a popular adolescent peer group widely admired for being cool—sharp dressers, good athletes, and successful with girls.

My outsider status derived from the fact that since 1972, unlike most of my peers of adolescence, I had spent my time pursuing a college education and an advanced degree, working and living in other parts of the state and country. Thus, when I began this research, one the one hand I was perceived as a homeboy who knew what was happening on the street. On the other hand, I was perceived as an outsider in that I possessed a college education and a white-collar job. I routinely turned down invitations to engage in certain insider-specific activities. I always graciously refused invitations, for example, to smoke marijuana and crack cocaine. Moreover, I was always sensitive to make sure that in my interactions with females, my actions could not reasonably be interpreted as oriented toward the pursuit of sexual relations.

My age also contributed to the perception of me as an outsider to those males who were 25 years old and younger. I was in my late twenties and early thirties during the time span in which I was directly involved in this research project. Thus, individuals 25 and under had not been a part of my adolescent cohort and generally did not possess any direct knowledge of my personal background as a homeboy.

The Interview Schedule

The interview schedule was designed to tap issues similar to those examined in prior studies conducted by Toch, Athens, Levi, Felson, and Ray and Simons.[12] The primary objective of the interview was to encourage a sample of black men to reconstruct violent confrontations in which they were involved. In previous studies this data-gathering approach had proven to be effective in helping researchers gain a better understanding of the intra- and interpersonal dynamics of violent confrontations;

> In order to understand a violent person's motives for violence, we must thus step into his shoes, and we must reconstruct his unique perspective, no matter how odd or strange it may be.[13]

Each respondent was asked to specify the following: (1) the precipitating factor that had led to the confrontation; (2) his feelings and attitudes as the confrontation unfolded; (3) the contribution of third parties; (4) his rationale for engaging in violent conduct; (5) whether he or his antagonist violated any social rules; (6) the influence of alcohol and drugs on the outcome of the incident; (7) how the confrontation could have been prevented; and (8) the post-incident effects of the incident on his routine activities associated with frequenting bars and bar settings (see the Appendix).

The interview schedule consisted of seven components: (1) introduction; (2) sequence of events; (3) personal orientation, meanings, and intentions; (4) alcohol and drug use; (5) post-incident effects; (6) violence prevention strategies. Each of these components is described below. Respondents' views on how the incidents in which they participated could have been prevented, however, are not discussed in the findings, primarily due to substantial replication of what they reported regarding rule violations as a precipitating factor.

Opening Statement

Prior to conducting each interview, I read the respondent a brief statement that specified the objectives of the study. I informed the respondent that the primary objective of the study was to examine the interpersonal dynamics of violent confrontations that occur between black males while frequenting bars and bar settings.

In addition, during the introductory component I indicated to the respondent that I wanted to analyze his personal account because I thought that his personal experience and perspective on interpersonal violence among black men represented an untapped source of first-hand information.

Finally, I informed the respondent that the interview was confidential and that his personal account would not be shared with any member of the local community.

Description of the Incident

The respondent was asked to describe an assault or homicide in which he had been one of the primary participants. During this component of the interview, I sought to gain information regarding his perception of the precipitating factor leading to violence, the behavioral sequences that constituted the basic structure of the interpersonal transaction, and the influence of third parties.

Personal Account for Use of Violence

The respondent was asked to describe his feelings during critical stages of the encounter that culminated in violence. He was asked to describe his reactions, for example, to insults, and threats, or physical assaults. In addition, the respondent was asked to discuss why he chose to engage in violence during a particular stage in the interaction between himself and his antagonist.

Third Parties

The respondent was asked to describe how third parties influenced the incidents in which they were involved. Emphasis was placed on uncovering how the respondent perceived the efforts of third parties to mediate or instigate the confrontation between he and his antagonist.

Alcohol and Drug Use

The respondent was asked to characterize the pharmacological effects of his antagonist's pre-incident alcohol or drug use. In addition, the respondent was asked to describe how alcohol or drugs influenced his own behavior and/or the behavior of his antagonist.

Post-Incident Effects

The respondent was asked to describe how his involvement in a violent confrontation in a bar or bar setting subsequently influenced his routine activities associated with frequenting bars and bar settings.

Violence-Prevention Strategies

The respondent was asked to comment on how the violent confrontation in which he participated could have been prevented. In addition, the respondent was asked to state his opinion on what needs to be done to reduce the high rates of violence among black men.

Validity and Reliability

I checked the validity of the interview schedule by consistently asking each respondent at the conclusion of the interview session to comment on whether he felt that the interview had been comprehensive. If he felt that I had failed to ask him about a critical issue, I encouraged him to express his views.

I did not employ any traditional strategies such as the test-retest method, the alternative form method, or the subsample method to test the reliability of the interview schedule. However, to insure that I was gathering data on violent confrontations that had occurred in bars and bar settings, I restricted my respondents from providing me with accounts of incidents that did not occur in bars or bar settings. In addition, I refused to listen to accounts of incidents in which one of the primary participants was either a woman or nonblack.

I checked validity or authenticity of each personal account primarily by its internal consistency. *Internal consistency* "refers to the degree to which the informant contradicts or corrects himself or gives apparently logically inconsistent or paradoxical information."[14] It refers to the truthfulness of the informant's account. In this study the truthfulness of each account was checked by assessing its internal consistency and by cross-comparison with personal accounts that have a similar focus. The utility and reliability of internal consistency checks has been affirmed by Paul and the Newsons, who report that an informant is unlikely to remain internally consistent if he is lying.[15]

External corroboration refers to "the degree to which the account may be matched against information relative to the event outside the immediate accounting situation."[16] In this study there was minimal external corroboration because most of the incidents involved were acts of nonfatal violence that had not been reported to the police. In a few cases the county prosecutor's office and the probation department was contacted.

Data Analysis

The accounts of a nonrandom sample of forty-one black men constitute the primary units of analysis in this study. The term *account* often refers to "a statement made by a social actor to explain unanticipated or untoward behavior."[17] Thus, when so defined, the term *account* refers to various neutralization techniques—for example, excuses or justifications—employed by individuals involved in problematic situations.

In analyzing the data I obtained through focused interviews with a sample of violent black men, however, the term *account* will also be used to refer to "the personal record of an event by the individual experiencing it, told from his point of view."[18] Therefore, in this study a distinction is made between *accounts* as techniques employed to neutralize or mitigate the perception of wrongdoing and *accounts* as informed statements made by the individuals whose experiences are under investigation.

Content Analysis

In order to condense and reinterpret the accounts, the data were analyzed through the application of the content-analysis technique. The primary purpose of content analysis is to condense voluminous qualitative data into meaningful explanatory categories.

To facilitate content analysis of the accounts, all the interviews were transcribed and their content analyzed in order to subcategorize the patterns into these content areas:

1. the major causes of violence among black men;
2. factors respondents considered to be the major causes of the violent confrontations in which they were involved;
3. interpersonal sequencing associated with violent confrontations in the bars and bar settings;
4. the characteristics of third-party intervention in violent confrontations in bars and bar settings;
5. how respondents refer to values, norms, and role-orientations associated with compulsive masculinity when providing accounts of their involvement in violent confrontations;
6. how respondents account for (excuse or justify) their involvement in violent confrontations;

7. how respondents associate pre-incident alcohol and/or drug consumption with their behavior or the behavior of their antagonists;

8. how participation in violent confrontations affects routine activities associated with frequenting bars and bar settings.

Although I was interested in examining all these content areas, I directed special attention toward categorizing respondents' references to compulsive masculinity norms and identifying the types of violence-prone black men involved in violent confrontations in bars and bar settings. The indexes I constructed to code and categorize these concerns are detailed in full below, as the Compulsive Masculinity Index and the Violence Propensity Index.

Compulsive Masculinity Index

In Chapter 4, I stated that a key premise of the integrated theoretical perspective underlying this study is that black males' efforts to enact compulsive masculinity role-orientations are major factors contributing to the high rates of violence among black men. Thus, a major content area that is analyzed in this study is their reference to values and norms associated with compulsive masculinity.

Norms have been generally defined as social rules or "group-supported definitions of expected behavior in specific situations."[19] Sociologists consider norms to be important because they often orient individuals' attitudes and behavior. Although there is a great deal of consensus among sociologists that norms have a direct impact on behavior, very few attempts have been made to directly measure the relationship between norms, norm violations, and the imposition of punitive sanctions for norm violations.

The Compulsive Masculinity Index described below has been designed to subcategorize those circumstances and situations for which lower-class black men believe local conduct norms condone the use of violence. To code the references to norms, I was guided by Meier's definition of norms as social rules that "identify behavior that 'ought to' or 'ought not' occur either in specific situations or at anytime or place."[20] This definition is based on a conceptualization of a norm as an evaluation of conduct as opposed to a norm as expected or predictable conduct. According to Meier, focusing on the evaluative meanings of norms is important because it sensitizes researchers to two important features of norms:

1. that norms are relative, that is, norms differ from one another according to the degree of condemnation they elicit; and

2. norms are usually linked to sanctions.

Thus, I examined the evaluative meaning of norms, from the perspective of violent black men, because I reject assumptions that suggest that all perceptions of norm violations give rise to punitive sanctions. By examining black men, I was able to extract how various contingencies and mitigating factors intervene between the definition of acts as norm violations and responses to those acts. According to Toch, "Ultimately, it is the individual who decides whether violence is to be eagerly adopted, casually rehearsed, or totally ignored."[21]

People evaluate norm violations both individually and collectively and both cognitively and behaviorally. Therefore, it is not unreasonable to assume that norms are reflected in and measurable from common discourse. Thus, the Compulsive Masculinity Index has been designed to subcategorize, from the perspective of black men, norms, norm violations, contingencies, and sanctions that give structure to motives, perceptions, meanings, and the sequence of events leading to violent confrontations among black men.

Another advantage of examining the evaluative meaning of norms is that it allows me to content-analyze the accounts for indications of the respondents' adherence to compulsive masculinity role orientations or other pro-violence norms. In addition, it facilitates my ability to subcategorize the respondents' claims that the incident was precipitated by their antagonists' adherence to compulsive masculinity or other pro-violence norms.

In constructing the Compulsive Masculinity Index, I relied on the work of Miller, Clark, Liebow, Hannerz, and Staples for descriptions of compulsive masculinity norms typically attributed to lower-class black males.[22] *Compulsive masculinity* is generally defined as a pattern of masculine behavior characterized by overt commitment to norms that emphasize toughness, autonomy, sexual conquest, manipulation, and thrill-seeking.

General Instructions

For each respondent's account, the content has been analyzed to determine if references to compulsive masculinity norms are present. References to a norm that appears to be salient relative to the sequence and events, excuses and justifications, and feelings and attitudes have been coded as primary. The major objective of this portion of the content analysis is to determine how and in what context black men refer to compulsive masculinity norms when providing an account of their behavior or the behavior of their antagonists regarding participation in violent confrontations. In the "Code" section, a brief description of each norm is provided, followed by a listing of situations that were used to provide guidance in determining whether references to compulsive masculinity norms were presented in the accounts.

Code

A. **Toughness—refers to a norm that encourages a willingness to use violence as a means of resolving interpersonal conflicts. Instances of this type are those in which the respondent expresses a concern with demonstrating his manhood through violent actions.**

A1. The respondent indicates that his involvement in a violent incident was precipitated by his antagonist's symbolic or overt display of toughness.

A2. The respondent indicates that his violent actions were precipitated by symbolic or overt displays of toughness engaged in by third parties.

B. **Autonomy—refers to a norm that defines manhood in terms of immunity to the orders and instructions of others. Instances to be denoted here are those said to have been precipitated by one of the participant's perceptions that he has been ordered to do something.**

B1. Violence as a reaction to orders and instructions.

B2. Violence as a reaction to being made to feel like a child.

C. **Sexual Conquest—refers to a norm in which manhood is defined in terms of sexual promiscuity and emotional and financial exploitation of females. Instances denoted here are those in which interpersonal conflicts emerge within the context of mutual pursuit and/or exploitation of females.**

C1. Violence as a jealous reaction.

C2. Violence as a retaliation for exploitation of a female relative or friend.

D. **Manipulation—refers to a norm that emphasizes exploitation of others through the use of one's wits. The instances denoted here are those in which respondents refer to exploitation actions as precipitating potentially violent or actual violent confrontations.**

D1. Violence as a reaction of feeling that someone is trying to exploit you.

E. **Thrill-Seeking—refers to a norm that associates manhood with participation in high-risk activities, such as hanging out on inner-city street corners and chronic use of alcohol and drugs, especially in bars, parking lots, poolrooms, gambling parlors, and on street corners. Instances denoted here are those in which respondents allude to alcohol and drug consumption, drug dealing, gambling, or hanging out as major factors contributing to their involvement in a potentially violent or actually violent confrontation.**

E1. Violence as an outcome of participating in high-risk activities.

Violence Propensity Index

A major dimension of this study is that it examines the motives and intentions of black men involved in violent confrontations. In the discussion of the findings, the accounts of the respondents are examined in terms of Toch's typology of violence-prone persons. The purpose of Toch's typology is to categorize the typical motives that characterize an individual's violent episodes and reflect his personality predisposition to engage in violent conduct.

I examined the accounts of violent black men to determine if those who are involved in violent confrontations in bars and bar settings are disproportionately represented in the types described by Toch.

General Instructions

For each incident describe, the content of the account was content-analyzed to determine if the violence-prone types described by Toch are applicable. In the "Code" section, each of Toch's violence-prone personality types is described, followed by additional indicators of situations in which the various types are salient.

Code

A. **Rep-Defending—refers to a category of persons who are influenced by public acclaim, encompassing the exercise of aggressive violence. Instances denoted here are those in which the individual's role or social position imposes a social obligation to engage in violent conduct.**

   A1. Violence as a reaction to the slightest provocation.
   A2. Violence as an expression of a particular social role.
   A3. Violence as a social obligation to satisfy the audience.

B. **Norm-Enforcing—refers to a self-assigned mission involving the use of violence on behalf of norms that the violent person sees as desirable. Instances denoted here are confrontations precipitated by the definition of certain actions as violating social norms.**

   B1. Violence in defense of other persons engaged in potentially violent or actual violent confrontations.

C. **Self-Image-Defending—refers to a tendency to use aggression as a form of retribution against people who the person feels have cast aspersions on his self-image. Instances denoted here are those in which the respondent reports that his violent actions were induced by threats to his self-image.**

   C1. Violence as a reaction to verbal insults.
   C2. Violence as a reaction to physical violence.

D. **Self-Image-Promoting—refers to the use of violence as a demonstration of one's worth, by persons who self-definition places emphasis on toughness and status. Instances denoted here involve efforts on the part of one combatant to demonstrate his worth at the expense of the other.**

   D1. Violence as an expression of a willingness to fight.
   D2. Violence in response to prearranged situations in which status is likely to be challenged.

D3. Interpersonal conflict if perceived as an opportunity to engage in violent conduct.

E. **Self-Defending—refers to a tendency to perceive other persons as sources of physical danger that require neutralization. Instances denoted here are those in which involvement in violent confrontations is explained as self-defense.**

E1. Violence as an effort to avoid physical harm.

F. **Pressure-Removing—refers to a propensity to explode in situations with which one is unable to deal. Instances denoted here are those in which a lack of verbal skills precludes an extended verbal confrontation.**

F1. Violence as a reaction to feeling that a more verbally skilled opponent is winning an argument.

G. **Bullying—refers to a orientation in which pleasure is obtained from the ability to instill fear in individuals uniquely susceptible to it. Instances denoted here are those in which individuals go out of their way to be unmerciful in violent situations.**

G1. Violence as a means of deriving satisfaction from the suffering of others.
G2. Violence as a means of generating fear in others.
G3. Violence as an instrument of gaining compliance from others.

H. **Exploitation—refers to a persistent effort to manipulate others into becoming unwilling tools of one's pleasure and convenience. Violence is used to enforce demands, or as backup when other people react against this effort. Instances denoted here are those precipitated by manipulation.**

H1. Violence as a means of facilitating efforts to take advantage of others.
H2. Violence as a reaction to manipulation.

I. **Self-Indulging—refers to a tendency to operate under the assumption that other people exist to satisfy one's own needs—with violence as a contingency of noncompliance. Instances denoted here are those in which an individual reacts violently when he perceives that his needs are not being satisfied.**

I1. Violence as a means of encouraging others to satisfy one's needs.

J. **Catharting—refers to a tendency to use violence to discharge accumulated internal pressure, or in response to recurrent angry feelings or moods. Instances denoted here are those that involve individuals who tend to encourage indiscriminate acts of violence.**

J1. Violence motivated by a desire to relieve tension and achieve peace of mind.

J2. Violence as a means of cheering oneself up.

J3. Occasions to engage in violence are arbitrarily selected.

Limitations

Several factors limit the generalizability of the findings reported in this study.

First, the sample comprises black men who have been involved in violent confrontations with other black men. Thus, the findings will not be easily generalizable to interpersonal violence that involves other racial/ethnic or gender configurations of violence participants.

Second, the sample comprises black men who volunteered to participate in the study. Thus, the findings reflect the views of a self-selected subsection of the available population of violent black men residing in the locale in which the study was conducted.

Third, because the majority of the incidents that the respondents reported involved nonfatal violence, it was difficult to provide external corroboration of the respondents' accounts.

Finally, the research was conducted in small city, located in upstate New York. According to the 1980 Census tracts, U.S. blacks represented 5,304 or 7.01 percent of that city's total population of 75,632. Most of the blacks under forty years old are first-, second-, or third-generation descendants of migrant workers who originally came to upstate New York from Alabama, Georgia, and Florida to work in local bean fields and apple orchards. Subsequently, these migrants remained in the area and secured employment as laborers in the textile mills, or as custodians or domestics.

Blacks in this community have not achieved significant economic gains since their arrival. For example, 47 percent of black families residing in this community earned incomes below the official U.S. poverty level in 1979.[23]

In the following chapters the intra- and interpersonal processes associated with violent confrontations between black men are discussed, based on their interpretation of their own experiences.

6

HANGING OUT

The meanings and definitions that black men associate with frequenting bars and bar settings are discussed in this chapter. In addition, the respondents' views of factors that contribute to interpersonal violence between black men in such settings are examined.

Hanging Out

Many of the men I interviewed spent a significant portion of their leisure time engaged in social interaction with others in bars and bar settings. To understand the cultural context in which violent confrontations occur among black men, I asked the respondents to discuss why they and their peers spent so much time in bars and bar settings. They generally perceived these settings as socially approved places to engage in sociability. However, they also viewed these settings as potentially dangerous places in which they were at risk of having their property, reputation, or physical safety threatened.

The term *hanging out* was used by the respondents to refer to a cluster of activities associated with frequenting bars and bar settings, including drinking, using drugs, pursuing women, talking to friends, playing cards, shooting pool, standing on street corners, and sitting in cars. Hanging out is a major feature of the lifestyle of lower-class black men.

When I asked respondents to explain their rationale for hanging out, they reported that black men hang out for a variety of reasons, including to socialize; to sell, purchase, or use drugs; to meet women; and to manipulate or exploit others.

Hanging Out to Socialize

The respondents believed that the high rate of unemployment among black men was primarily responsible for the inordinate amount of time that they and their peers spent patronizing bars and standing on street corners. They saw unemployment as the catalyst and foundation for the institution of hanging out and the various routine activities associated with hanging out in bars and bar settings:

> I: What does it mean to be out here? What are people doing when they are hanging out?
> Lee: There's nothing else to do. This is it, for amusement and a chance to get to see most of the people in town without going to their homes to visit them. Just hanging out, socializing.

> Don Juan: Probably no work, probably women . . . but I think it's work. I think that's what State Street is all built up on.
> I: What's that?
> Don Juan: No work. They ain't got no work, so you come on South Street and get drunk just to hang out. You cause trouble or whatever.

Table 6–1 illustrates the primary income sources of the forty-one respondents.

The social activities associated with hanging out in bars and bar settings generally occur within the context of primary peer groups. Some respondents were very sensitive to the differences that existed between various peer groups. For example:

> Lee: Well, let's take our group. We are not real cool, but we have a level head. We are a mediocre group. Then you got the wino guys. They are like alcoholics. They get drunk all day and night. Then you got the violent guys that hang across the block, who like to rob and beat everyone that comes through the neighborhood. Then you got your drug addicts who hang on the other corner. Then you got your standbyers. They aren't in a specific group or area.
> I: Are they lame [square]?
> Lee: No, they are learning.
> I: How old are they?
> Lee: They are between sixteen and twenty-one.
> I: So they don't know what route they are going to take?

Table 6–1
Primary Income Sources of Respondents

Respondent	Welfare	Minimum Wage Employment	Middle-Income Employment	Dependent on Mother
B.B.	X			
Chast		X		
Derrick	X			
Terry B.		X		
Big Bob	X			
Brown		X		
Dox	X			
Turner	X			
Houston		X		
Rigsby	X			
Mike	X			
Hicks	X			
Hawkins			X	
Harry B.	X			
Patterson				X
Kessler	X			
Don Juan	X			
Cecil	X			
Hendricks	X			
Lender	X			
Frank			X	
Uzell	X			
Juan W.				X
Johnny B.	X			
Germ		X		
Lee		X		
Willie B.	X			
Paul		X		
Holt		X		
Troy	X			
Mac			X	
Lonzo			X	
Walker			X	
Butch	X			
Watson	X			
Joey				X
Washington	X			
McKenzie		X		
Carr	X			
Sonny			X	
Jesse			X	
Total	22	9	7	3

Lee: Yeah. They indulge here and dab there. They are here learning to do the wrong things.

I: What would be some of the wrong things to learn?

Lee: The route for drinking, the route for drugs, and the disposition of men toward women.

I: What are the attitudes toward women among the men who hang out?

Lee: Man is dominant. Man rules. Man should be the one that be able to make his say-so and it be that. Give me say-so to a woman. Put no value on how she feels about any situation or anything.

Hanging Out for Drugs and Women

A significant feature of the routine activities associated with hanging out in black bars and bar settings involves getting high on alcohol or drugs and chasing women. According to the men I interviewed, these activities are an important feature of the enforced leisure they ascribe to joblessness:

Mac: There's nothing else to do. They can't find a job because half of them ain't went to school. So they're out of a job—they ain't gonna get no job. If they do get one, they're only going to work like a week, get a check, and quit. There ain't nothing for them to do but hang on State Street till the first—get their check. Everybody parties on the first. But that's all they can look forward to. There's no jobs, there's nothing for the people to get involved in.

I: So what are they involved in?

Mac: Drugs, partying—that's it. That's basically it. And making kids.

I: What do you think is the attraction to hanging out?

Paul: It's the get-high part, I guess. That's the only thing I can see. You wake up in the morning, you get high, you can go to sleep high. Wake up, figure out where you are gong to borrow three dollars from. I hung out with Ray for about eighteen months when I was out of work. I moved out from my house, and we hung out. I mean we would go to bed stoned, wake up in the morning, and we would hustle all day long, just enough to get some beer, wine, and to get some coke. We would get fucked up and start all over again the next fucking morning. I did that for eighteen months.

I: Why do brothers hang out? Why do the brothers spend so much time hanging out on the streets and in bars like Galaxy and Frank's?

Troy: Women, women, man!

I: Women?

Troy: It is either women or drugs. . . . It's drugs. If you got drugs, you get women.

I: Why?

Troy: It's what the women want.

I: They want drugs?

Troy: There you go! You give them drugs—you can spend as many days as you want with them. If you don't have the drugs, you just got to go with the natural rap—if you can talk to them to get them to take you home.

I: I like that term, "a natural rap." As opposed to what—a drug rap?

Troy: It is either a natural rap or a trick. If you are giving a female money or other things and it's not your lady, that is what you are doing, tricking. That's what it is. That is what most everybody is doing now.

I: What?

Troy: Selling drugs, and when they want to get laid up, snort this, smoke that, let's go.

Abuse of cocaine and crack by black women is having a substantial effect on how heterosexual relationships are initiated in bars and bar settings. A part-time drug dealer reports:

Lee: I don't see how they could sell themselves just like that. But I've been approached. Last night there must have been about a whole half a dozen talking about "Can I take you home?" Just because I brought over a package. But they know me better than that. Shit, I ain't no trick, and I ain't about to be no trick. I see a lot of good decent girls just throw their shit down the drain. Man, I mean the guy with the package might be an old junkie bum, and this nice woman will give her whole self up to this guy.

I: Are a lot of women hooked, or do they just like to do the drug for fun?

Lee: I think the women got it worse than the men. They want it every day. They are more naive in this area, and they seem to be weaker. And once they get under the influence of drugs, it seems like they submit themselves to anything. But that is true. These women are selling themselves like wild, and it don't make any sense. It is unbelievable how easy it is for them to be taken advantage of just for some white powder.

Hanging Out to Manipulate and Exploit Others

According to Goffman, "there are extraordinary niches in social life where activity is so markedly problematic and consequential that the participant is likely to orient himself to fatefulness prospectively, perceiving in these terms what it is that is taking place."[1] An activity is defined as problematic and consequential when it has reputational implications.

Black men patronize bars, after-hours joints, and other street-corners settings primarily to engage in various social activities with their relatives and friends. While they tend to use these places to facilitate sociability, however, they are also aware of fateful consequences that may occur while frequenting them.

> *Brown:* Bars fascinate. They have a tendency of doing things to people, especially if the crowd is right. It depends on who it is. They might have had a bad night last night. A bar's a bad place for people because you bring all your problems in the bar. If you had a fight with your old lady, you see your best friend in the bar, you discuss it. Next thing you know, some other nigger done got in your conversation, now you gonna fight him. But that's the way bars are. I don't give a damn what bar it is, there's always some nigger in there that don't like you, gonna say something bad about you, and one thing leads to another.

The perception of bars and bar settings as fateful social settings was partially related to the respondents' belief that it is very common for black men who hang out to attempt to exploit or manipulate other men. They commonly used the phrase "trying to get over" to refer to individuals engaging in actions directed toward manipulating or exploiting another person.

> *Lee:* You have to watch out for getting yourself in a bad situation. Like getting too intoxicated, or getting too high, or even just making a slight mistake with anything of value to you, like jewelry, money, or any personal thing that has any value to you. You have to be real careful about it. That's the main thing you have to watch out for— being taken advantage of, not only by outsiders and strangers but also by your best friends and your own family.

Fatefulness was also linked to activities associated with drug-trafficking in and around bars and bar settings. Drug dealers are particularly sensitive to the envy and hostility that their economic success and high profile status engenders among their peers:

> *Lee:* Me, myself, I like selling drugs to make an extra buck.
> *I:* Marijuana or coke?
> *Lee:* Cocaine. But jealousy sets in. They [some of the other drug dealers] feel that I be taking from them. But I feel that I be serving justice because I know what they be running around here, and it be gar-

bage. When a man works hard for his money, he wants the best out of his money. I feel that I give the best.

The bars and bar settings in this community were used extensively to facilitate the sale and purchase of illegal drugs. Moreover, many of the respondents believed that because of the persuasiveness of the "get over" mentality and drug-trafficking, bars and bar settings were commonly the scene of drug-related conflicts. For example:

Mac: People are going to try you, especially when you're dealing drugs, because they figure you want the money. You want to get paid, so . . . say like, I cop from you . . . say I cop once or twice. . . . Now the second time I go back, I'm gonna try you. I'm gonna try to get over. I'm not gonna give you what you ask. I'm gonna give you what I feel I can get over and get it cheaper for me.

I: Like instead of twenty-five, you give me twenty-one?

Mac: Yeah, or fifteen. Because I'm trying to get over. I figure, I done been there one time, give it to me for fifteen. You got to get me out of your face. And actually, I'm getting over. If you get popped, the man, when he says that bail money, he ain't gonna say, "well, just give me what you got." If you can't make the bail, you're gonna sit out there till you make it. And the dope dealers today, they're starting to realize this. I'm out here busting my ass—if I get popped, ain't nobody gonna help me. So I'm not giving it up for them, I'm not giving it up. "If anybody rips me off, I'm gonna kill somebody." That's the way they think. A lot of people get hurt. It's not like when we came up. Of course, all that drug stuff wasn't around.

Guns on the Street

Many of the respondents believed that it is very common for men who hang out to either carry weapons or have easy access to weapons. These beliefs contribute to the definition of black bars and bar settings as dangerous places:

Mac: Years ago when we use to hang out, it was fights and stuff, but it was mostly fights with fists. You bet me, I beat you. Now it's guns. You get into a fight, and you'll get shot. You can get killed out there over what—because you spilled a beer on my leg, or you stepped on my feet, or I picked up the wrong cigarettes.

I: Are a lot of people carrying weapons?

Mac: Yes, weapons, guns.

I: Why are people carrying guns?

Mac: Because you never know what's going to happen out there in the street. You get in an argument—just like myself—I don't carry nothing. I get in an argument with a guy, I'm ready to hold my fists. He pulls out a gun, and I could be totaled. If he blasts me, I'm finished. He's probably feeling the same way, he don't know what I got.

A salient theme in respondents' accounts of black bars and bar settings as dangerous places was that the technology of conflict has changed over time, from fist fights to armed confrontations. Carrying weapons into bars and bar settings reflected a willingness to resort to lethal means to avoid being disrespected and/or physically assaulted:

Lee: We are all growing up now, and we don't feel that we should have to box and wrestle with nobody or be disrespected. Even me myself, I'm not going to box or wrestle anybody anymore. If somebody do something to me, I might not say shit to them. I might get on up and they kick me in my ass, and I'm going to walk away. But I will return to do something.
  I: When you are hanging out on the street, do you generally have quick access to your weapon?
Lee: Yes. I have access to my weapons. I got me a hunting knife, with a blade eleven or twelve inches long. And I got a .357 Magnum with a clip in my vehicle.
  I: So brothers are carrying weapons because they think other brothers are carrying weapons?
Lee: Yeah. They know that other brothers are carrying weapons. I carry weapons just to keep up, just to keep balance.

Rules of the Street

Rules of conduct are an important source of constancy and patterning of behavior. According to Goffman:

> Rules of conduct impinge on the individuals in two general ways: directly, as obligations, establishing how he is morally constrained to conduct himself; indirectly, as expectations how others are morally bound to act in regard to him.[2]

Social interaction in bars and bar settings is guided by such rules of conduct. To gain an understanding of the rules that were predominant in the bars and bar settings that the respondents frequented, I asked them to list and describe these "rules of the street." I also asked the respondents what advice they would give to a young boy who was just beginning to hang out in the bars and bar settings.

"Mind Your Own Business"

"Mind your own business" was the rule of conduct that was cited most often by the respondents. The purpose of this rule is to regulate interpersonal relations within black bars and bar settings. In addition, adherence to this rule reinforces a definition of manhood in which men are supposed to be independent and immune from external interference:

> *I:* When men come into the bars or they're hanging out on the street, how are they supposed to behave? What are the rules of the street?
>
> *Dox:* Well, you mind your own business. I mean, that's common sense—leave people alone. I don't know you, you don't know me, let's leave it at that. You wanna get to know me, it's a way to do it. I don't want to be bothered with you. . . . I mean, long as you are being a gentleman, I ain't got no problem . . . unless you know me, ah . . . you just never know what's on somebody else's mind. That's why you don't bother people. I mean, you may have problems. You may be ill, your mother or your kids may be ill, you may not have no food, your family's home, your baby need Pampers, so you leave people alone. You respect people, and you get respect.

One respondent applied the "mind your own business" rule to banter and conversation among friends. For example, he believed that it was not good to allow people to draw him into conversations that were ongoing prior to his arrival at the bar:

> *Brown:* When you come in somewhere and the conversation done already been started, but when you get there, it's like, "All right, Brown, I'm gonna relate it to you. I'm gonna let you know what's happening." I don't want to know. Don't give me no parts of that, I wasn't here. As far as I'm concerned, I don't want to take the weight and be in the middle of something. You done got away walking out the door. Now I'm stuck with this. It happens so quickly.

"Avoid Trouble"

"Avoid trouble" is another significant rule of conduct that respondents associated with interpersonal conflict. This rule is related to the "mind your own business" rule. For example, in the bar and street-corner context where these men spent most of their leisure time, to mind someone else's business was representative of not adhering to the "avoid trouble" rule. The potential for encountering trouble is omnipresent for black men whose lifestyles are based on spending an inordinate amount of time in sexual promiscuity, chronic substance abuse, and hanging out in bars and on the streets:

    I: What would you tell the young boys about hanging out?

  Troy: "Come on out and enjoy yourself. Don't look for no trouble. Takes a better man to walk away. Might get into one fight too many. It might cost your own life, over a silly-ass nigger out here in the street." I like hanging out. A lot of times I come out, sit here and say, "I'm tired of this," and go home. Just stay away from them. There are a lot of ignorant people out here who don't listen. . . . Like to walk away from all of this. It's not worth it. You know?

  Mike: I would tell him to be careful out there in the streets, don't be getting too intoxicated, watch who you be with, try to hang with the right people.

    I: Who are the right people, and who are the wrong people?

  Mike: It's hard to determine, man. Because you don't know who's going to do what out here.

  Butch: Everything that shine ain't gold. Because you will probably see this person pull out their wallet, and you might see those hundreds in there. Because you see that money don't mean you have to put your hands on it. That man go about his business, and you keep on doing what you have to do to go about your business. You want to be a man, you act like a man. You want to be a kid, you act like a kid. On the streets you can't act like no kid, you got to be a man, you got to be responsible, you got to know what you're doing out there.

Young Boys, Drugs, and New Rules

Several of the men who were over thirty years old expressed the view that the rules of the street were changing, especially among the "young boys"—that is, males between 16 and 25 years of age. The new rules being promoted by the young boys de-emphasize the importance of possessing women and appear to take women and sex for granted. Drugs, making money, and power are their predominant concerns. Consequently, many older respondents believe that the young boys are a lot more violent than they themselves were when they were young boys hanging out in the streets:

  Brown: If they don't know you, they'll shoot you down like you ain't nobody. And you don't really be doing nothing, you just trying to show them the right way of what's happening.

The young boys were described as being responsible for the introduction of a new drug culture that emphasized making money and a willingness to resort to violence as a means of settling disputes:

> *I:* Is there a lot of suspiciousness out here, distrust about people?
> *Johnny B.:* Yeah.
> *I:* Why is that?
> *Johnny B.:* A new kind of drug culture has moved into the scene.

> *I:* Do you think the younger generation is more violent than our generation of the late 1960s?
> *Mac:* Much more.
> *I:* What do you think that's attributed to?
> *Mac:* Drugs.

> *Paul:* They don't care nothing about nobody. I think they would kill their momma.
> *I:* Do you think that has something to do with the way they are brought up or what?
> *Paul:* No. I think it's the way they hang. It's the crowd they hang out with. Everybody wants to get fast.

Moreover, when confronted with interpersonal conflict, the young boys were perceived as less likely than older men to talk it out or fist fight:

> *I:* What are some of the main rules of the street in terms of how a man is supposed to behave out here?
> *Jesse:* The rules are very much changed. We use to talk shit about "your ass." The young brothers now are talking about "popping a cap in your ass." I don't understand their rule, but I understand what popping a cap means.

Another aspect of the new rules and the new drug culture is that the young boys seemed to show less interest in women than the older men. According to the older respondents, the young boys were romantically and sexually involved with females, but they did not fight over them to the same degree that the older men had when they were young boys:

> *Johnny B.:* These young boys don't care about women. I never see them with a main woman.
> *I:* So there's less fighting over women?
> *Johnny B.:* Right.
> *I:* So the young boys are more likely to fight over the fact that somebody sold them some bad drugs.

Johnny
 B.: Right. That's a shame, too. They're out here just making babies.

The older men also described the young boys as lacking respect for themselves and others:

> *Jesse:* You've got to respect yourself, and by you respecting yourself, you are showing others respect. You got people that just don't know nothing about respect and don't care nothing about respect. They don't give a shit about respect.
>
> *I:* Do you think that's more common among the young boys out here?
>
> *Jesse:* That's where it's coming from, the young guys. It's a whole new program.
>
> *I:* What is the new program for the young boys?
>
> *Jesse:* These young boys, they don't want to do nothing—they don't even want to go to school. All they want to do is break in, steal, and do drugs—that's all. The majority of these young boys are raising themselves. Their parents don't care what they do.

Causes of Violence

The men that I interviewed were very much aware of the fact that bars and bar settings that constitute the street-corner context are often the scene of violent confrontations between black men. When asked to describe major factors contributing to interpersonal violence between black men, the respondents cited the following factors most frequently: drugs; women and romantic competition; unemployment and economic jealousy; disrespect; and alcohol intoxication.

Trying to "Get Over": Drugs and Other Games

"Getting over" involves a wide range of behavior and objectives, including: securing money through the use of one's wits, having sex with another man's wife or girlfriend, denigrating another person's social status or self-image, stealing something, manipulating a gambling situation, or winning a verbal argument or a physical confrontation.

For a man to be a victim of another man's "get over" strategy defines him as a loser in the public mind of the street-corner culture. Knowledge of the man's victimization may lead to light banter and ridicule, and it may even increase the man's desirability as a target for future acts of exploitation:

> *Don Juan:* It's so many people getting over on each other. One person

will beat this person, and the next person that just got beat, he gonna try to beat another person. So that's going to lead to conflict.

    I: Why are so many people out here trying to beat each other? Why is that?

Don Juan: I guess trying to get power, trying to get more respect from another person.

As this passage implies, routine activities related to getting over or exploiting others may lead to a variety of interactive sequences. For example, the vanquished person may attempt to reestablish his reputation by doing some "getting over" on his own.

As a factor contributing to violence, trying to "get over" was usually mentioned in the context of drug-trafficking. Selling drugs increases a man's risk of becoming a target of men who are prone to manipulate or exploit others:

Mac: Drug-trafficking is automatic trouble. Right from jump street. If you're trafficking and use drugs, that's trouble right off the bat. Because now at that time, you either set yourself up for a rip-off ... somebody's trying to rip you off ... or you're selling to undercover cops. It's trouble either way, it's trouble. But besides the violence, you have to protect yourself. People will try to rip you off. There's violence there. A lot of people have been getting shot—killed—between that thing, drugs. The trafficking or the selling or the buying, all of it, none of it's good.

    I: How do drugs cause fights?

Jesse: Well, you got people out here distributing it. The people making the sale and keeping the money are getting the man's product and telling him he got ripped off.

    I: Are you saying the drug dealers are trying to beat the drug dealers?

Jesse: Right.

    I: The drug dealer wants his money, and they're not giving up the money.

Jesse: Yeah. When he come for his money, they ain't got his money nor the product.

    I: Do you think there are more fights over drugs today than there are over women?

Mac: I think there's more fights over drugs than women. There's more violence over drugs. Half of the guys don't care about girls, they just want drugs. I think most of the fights got something to do with drugs, or somebody getting fast or somebody stealing something.

Women, Romantic Competition, and Jealousy

Romantic competition and jealousy are another major cause of violent confrontations between black men. In the account that follows, for example, a self-styled Don Juan illustrates how the successful enactment of "the player of women" image may lead to violent confrontations as a result of the envy of one's less fortunate peers:

Don Juan: What it boils down to, in my situation, it comes from females and what type of clothes you've got. A lot of brothers want to have these things, but they can't get these things because they are on some type of drug where it don't let them get that. They got to have that drug before they get these types of things. Or they don't have a conversation to pull together to get a lady.

I: You said you think that a lot of brothers dislike you because you have a lot of women. How do you know that?

Don Juan: They tell me.

I: They tell you what?

Don Juan: That "I don't like you." "You think you tough, you got a lot of females around here!" And that's what leads to fights once in a while, not all the time.

I: Would you say that one of the goals—one of the objectives of some of the brothers that hang out is to have a lot of women?

Don Juan: Yeah.

I: So they get upset when they see somebody else being successful in getting a lot of women and they haven't been able to do that?

Don Juan: Yes.

I: Do you think they spend a lot of time trying to get women?

Don Juan: Yes.

I: So if they spend a lot of time, what's the problem?

Don Juan: They spend a lot of time and don't get nothing. That leads to problems for another brother that do have a lot.

The termination of a romantic relationship enhances the likelihood of a violent confrontation between black men. It is not uncommon for a woman to manipulate a situation in order to publicly assert her independence from a husband or boyfriend or to symbolically demonstrate her involvement with a new man:

Troy: You go to a bar. You talk to a woman. She happens to be somebody else's woman. But now, she didn't tell you that. Even if she used to be somebody else's woman. Everybody hangs out in the same places, so you run across each other. Some dude don't want you talking to his ex, or some dude don't want you talking to a woman he wants to talk to.

I: So competition for women is significant?

Troy: I think it is a primary factor.

In some situations, the new man will take his cues from the woman and proactively assist her in her efforts to publicly terminate a romantic relationship:

Hicks: You gotta lot of women that's trying to get rid of their old man. And they see you, and they know you more or less as the type of guy that will kick ass, and they say, "I'm gonna use this guy to get rid of him." So she's sitting up there in the bar . . . "Hey baby, you look good to me. Can I buy you a drink?" Whereas normally you would be offering to buy her one. And she sits there and says blah, blah, blah. And says, "I've been trying to get away from this man and near you for the longest time. I know you ain't scared of him. And just think of what I can do for you." You sit there and have a few drinks. And she keep looking up at me just long enough. . . . And like, he calls you up.

I: Who calls you up?

Hicks: The brother calls you up. He says, "Yo, homeboy, the woman is through with you. She don't want nothing else to do with you." And bing, let's get it on. And to the victor goes the spoils. You know, the winner takes all. And that is a constant thing, especially around in our area, like State Street. Like every other weekend you see this happening.

Violence was also attributed to women being sexually unfaithful after raising expectations of fidelity:

I: How do females cause these fights?

Johnny B.: Playing games. "I ain't fucking nobody but you"—playing games like that. "I swear to God, I ain't going with nobody but you."

Jesse: The ladies cause a great deal of this conflict between the guys. She mess with one guy, and then you have this girl messing with another guy, and when they happen to meet, there's a conflict right there. He's thinking it's his woman, and the other guy is thinking it's his woman. And she got them both fooled.

While black women may self-consciously construct situations that lead black men to engage in violent confrontations precipitated by romantic competition and jealousy, it is much more common for the jilted man to initiate violence against the other man as a result of experiencing anger and hurt over the woman's decision to terminate the relationship. Losing a woman to another man may also pose a threat to a man's personal and public identity as a man. For example, many of the respondents associated manhood with dominance of one's woman and children. Losing control over one's woman and children could precipitate a great deal of animosity and hostility toward the girlfriend or wife's new man:

> *Hicks:* Nine times out of ten, the woman that he lost is to his best friend or to one of his good associates. Those are the only type of people that can hurt you—the people who are close to you. A guy who sees your situation, and he's been waiting for an opportunity to get into your woman's pants or whatever and he was always a good messenger to her. "You're just gonna have to get rid of him, you know. I wouldn't say it directly to him, but I'm just trying to let you know. I'm trying to be a friend here." And then she starts confiding in him, telling him everything. Now he knows more or less how he's gonna set things up to bring you down completely.
>
> *I:* Is he trying to bring you down, or is he just trying to get to the woman?
>
> *Hicks:* He's trying to bring you down, period. If he gets to the woman, that's half with him. But then, moving into your house, taking over—he's inherited everything you possess. Your kids—'cause the woman's gonna keep the kids—now your kids are callin' this guy daddy. It's enough to blow your socket, man.
>
> *I:* So that can be a major cause of violence?
>
> *Hicks:* It is a major cause around here. And it is constant around here because the brothers know if you are a player or a good hustler, you are normally out on the street most of the time. And your so-called friends find out that you're not home, they shoot directly to your crib.

Unemployment and Economic Jealousy

Earlier in this chapter, I noted that many of the respondents regarded unemployment as the catalyst and foundation for the specific style of hanging out engaged in by lower-class black males. In addition, some respondents felt that unemployment is a major cause of violence among black males. These respondents tended to associate being unemployed with being frustrated, desperate, and angry. That is, they believed that unemployment contributed to the emergence of an emotional state that substantially impeded the consideration of nonviolent alternatives in interpersonal conflict:

Jesse: Every time they go out to look for a job, people give them the runaround. Nobody's producing nothing. These guys ain't got nothing to do, and they got to get some kind of income coming in. They need some kind of money. They taking from each other.

   I: Taking what?

Jesse: Material things. Like breaking in houses, taking their TVs, their VCRs, taking their material things, or selling it for little or nothing. And then this person telling this other person where his stuff is—it creates a vicious cycle.

Paul: It don't take much to get them set off. If you ain't got a job and you ain't working, you got to go buy some clothes, so you have to hustle, and it's going to cost you damn near all of that hustle. Once you get to that bar, you probably have just enough to get yourself one decent drink, or buy you something cheap. Cheap Thunderbird or some Mad Dog and get half cocked before you get to the bar. You are already on a short fuse when you have been turned down by two or three people for jobs. 'Cause I knew when I wasn't working, I couldn't even get a job at McDonald's. It's rough when they tell you they aren't hiring when they got a big sign that says they are hiring. So you say, "Fuck it," and you walk down the street and hustle. Then you get a couple of dollars, and you can start drinking.

The respondents perceived the lack of adequate economic resources as being frustrating and as imposing limits on a black man's ability to fully engage in routine activities associated with manhood. The term *economic jealousy* has been introduced to characterized respondents' references to how some black men internalize envy and express hostility toward men who appear to be more economically advantaged than themselves.

Lee: There is a lot of jealousy in black neighborhoods. A lot of brothers envy other brothers for different reasons. Like, if he work and you don't work. The guy who works can go and approach different females, and the other guy can't. He always has his own, to supply his own way. His own cash. He can buy his own liquor. If he wants to smoke marijuana, he can smoke his own marijuana. And a lot of guys, they just hold grudges against people.

Paul: Some of them will never work. They ain't got nothing to do all day except hang out, smoke, and get high. When Saturday night comes, that is all they look for and don't want to know nothing about a guy that's got an honest job and who can come into the bar and buy a lady a drink. So there is bad feelings right there. . . .

There is a lot of pressure between guys that work and those that don't work. Like I said, when you go to a bar and a guy just has enough to buy himself a drink and not enough to buy a lady a drink. It's kind of rough because drinks are expensive.

Economic jealousy may motivate a man who lacks economic resources and material possessions to threaten or challenge the economically stable man by pursuing his wife or girlfriend. In the passage below the respondent describes knowledge of a man's involvement with women other than his wife as something that can be used to disrupt or destabilize the economically stable man:

> *Jesse:* Take for instance, a guy that's got a nice car, a home, a family man. These guys will relate a message, send rumors—so-and-so out messing out around here, doing this, doing that—making sure it gets back home. They will try to break up homes. These guys will break up a home as quick as a cop will pull his pistol. They don't care.
>
> *I:* Why are they doing this?
>
> *Jesse:* Resentment. Disrespect. No respect for you.
>
> *I:* Is it because they don't have any respect for you, or do they want what you got?
>
> *Jesse:* For a while they would want what you got, until they get you broken up. Once they get you out the picture, then they gone on about their business—laughing and talking.

Disrespect

The failure to show respect is another factor that the respondents listed in response to the question: What causes serious arguments and fights among black men? Disrespect was typically defined as a deliberate insult or aggressive action that was unwarranted.

Disrespect was a core issue in terms of how black men evaluate each others' behavior, especially behavior that leads to interpersonal violence:

> *I:* What causes most fights between guys hanging out in bars?
>
> *Chast:* Totally misunderstanding each other, and probably lack of respect for their fellow men or fellow person. Nobody likes to be disrespected, but I see it happens to us more often.
>
> *I:* Do you think the guys who hang out are very sensitive to being disrespected?
>
> *Chast:* Yeah, that's a big part of their ego.
>
> *I:* Would any little hint of disrespect cause a fight?
>
> *Chast:* Defensive shields would come up, I would say. You would be on your guard. You would think about it.

    I: Would you start thinking about getting ready to fight?

Chast: Getting ready to do a verbal or physical battle.

    I: What would be an example of disrespect that typically leads to violence?

Chast: A guy walks up to another guy—they could be friends, most of the time they are friends—and take his money.

    I: Take his money from where?

Chast: Off the bar. Like, I have twenty dollars' change on the bar, [you say,] "Hey, I want a drink," you pull the money and pay the bartender. Most people think that is being disrespectful.

Jesse: Say you're in the street—a guy can just step on your feet. He don't have the courtesy to say, "Excuse me, man, I'm sorry." That makes you mad: "Hey, man, can't you see you just stepped on my feet?" The first thing he gone do is jump off with something snotty. That ticks them off. It don't take much to start anything out here in these streets.

Disrespect was also associated with actions that limit a man's ability to function in an autonomous manner:

Lou: The main thing is just respecting each other. You got to have space. If we don't get that space, pressure builds up, and that's when you have conflict.

Disrespecting a Woman

The respect-disrespect standard was also evident with reference to violent confrontations about women. Respondents believed, for example, that violence would likely occur in situations in which an antagonist ignored the signs that another man had staked a claim on a particular woman:

Paul: You are with your young lady, and this guy says, "Give the young lady a drink." That kind of shit, you know. You go into the bathroom and a guy will send your lady a drink while you ain't there—disrespecting shit.

Chast: You be with your wife or your old lady, and a guy approaches your old lady in a manner not fitting the situation. Like kissing your old lady or grabbing your old lady's ass.

One of the major reasons lower-class blacks frequent bars and bar settings is to initiate heterosexual relationships. Thus, it is very common for black men to approach women in these settings. There are occasions, however, when these encounters result in the man translating disappointment into anger at a woman if he does not like the quality of her response to him. Disrespecting a woman in a bar or bar setting was listed among the rule violations that contribute to violent confrontations between black men:

> *Brown:* If you don't know a woman, I'd advise anyone to be careful. Say what you've got to say, but don't get indignant. There's a way of saying things, getting your point across, without getting violent or getting indignant. You can ask a lady something, and if she says, "I think that's personal," you should walk off. You cut the conversation. A lot of guys in the bar, they don't want to cut the conversation. They go from one extreme to another. They say, "Okay, bitch. You think you're stuck up, you think you're cute"—there you go. Now you done involved her husband or whoever.

Alcohol and Violence

Chronic alcohol use is very common among lower-class black males, particularly those who spend an inordinate amount of time in bars and bar settings. While the men I interviewed believe that violence among black men is primarily caused by drug disputes, conflict over women, and disrespect, alcohol intoxication was also cited as a causal factor.

In the accounts in which respondents cited alcohol intoxication as a factor contributing to interpersonal violence, they primarily emphasized how the pharmacological effects of alcohol cause individuals to act in an aggressive manner in a conflict-ridden situation:

> *Butch:* When you put that alcohol in your system, an "S" grows on your chest like Superman. Liquor makes you get bigger than what you are. You feel like you can whip the world.

> *Paul:* Most black guys wait until they start drinking, they got that liquid confidence. . . .

Alcohol intoxication was also associated with committing rule violations that lead to interpersonal violence among black men:

> *Hicks:* You came out to drink, or otherwise you could have stayed at home. After a few shots, it's either you approaching somebody else's woman or he is approaching yours because they happen to see her from the other side of the room and she appealed to them.
> *I:* Are you saying alcohol motivates people to start pursuing other people's women?
> *Hicks:* Yes, all the time. And quite naturally the guy will try to stop you and say, "Hey, that's my woman." And then the other guy is

waiting to hear something from the woman, and she figures she doesn't have to say anything because her old man is explaining it to you. But he overlooks that and just disrespects that and say, "To hell with you, man." And before you know it, you got conflict. And it's on from there. Nine times out of ten he's armed, you're armed, and somebody's hurt. Either shot, cut, or stabbed.

Drinking After Hours

According to several respondents, alcohol-related violence is frequently associated with hanging out and drinking in or immediately outside of after-hours joints:

> *Germ:* After-hour drinking is bad. That's why they got a law. Ninety percent of the time, when you do look at people that do get killed, it's after hours. . . . They get way more intoxicated after hours. It don't take much for them to go off. They be so full of that drink, and the least little thing—they go off. They want to fight.

Three after hours joints were frequently mentioned as places in which violent confrontations occurred. All of the respondents regarded Frank's as the most violent after-hours joint and more violent than any of the licensed bars. Drinking after hours was cited as a major factor contributing to the large number of violent incidents occurring at Frank's:

> *I:* How would you describe Frank's?
>
> *Lee:* Frank's? Vietnam. Anything might happen in Frank's. Frank's ain't safe to go into. You take a risk when you walk through the door.
>
> *I:* Why is that?
>
> *Lee:* It's a after-hours joint. After all the other joints close, we are left with Frank's. Now it's three or four o'clock in the morning. You can still get any kind of booze you want. You can get a beer, if you want a beer. You can get any kinds of drugs, if you want drugs. Then they are gambling in back. You got to look at the schedule. It's four o'clock in the morning, and a guy done been out the whole night before. And he is pretty well juiced up, tempers are flaring. And everybody is carrying a weapon when they go in there mostly. And there is always a risk that you might get cut or get shot or mistaken for the wrong guy. Frank's is Vietnam.

Another respondent offered a similar characterization of Frank's:

> *Paul:* We call it little Cambodia.
>
> *I:* Why?
>
> *Paul:* That's the war zone. You go down to Frank's place, you got to be

drunk, half drunk, or half crazy. I like hanging out down there, but I don't know which one I am.

In addition to the pharmacological effects of after-hours drinking, violence at Frank's was attributed to the type of crowd who hangs out at Frank's and the bar owner's willingness to use violence to enforce the rules of his establishment:

> *Lee:* Frank's is very different from other bars because you got a owner who doesn't mind putting his bat on you if you get belligerent or out of place. Not because you think you are out of place, but because he thinks you are. So you are in trouble there. You have to be careful when you go through Frank's.
>
> *I:* Some people say you are pretty safe in Frank's.
>
> *Lee:* Right. He won't let you get totally taken advantage of in his place. You might get taken advantage of outside, but not in his place. He is not going to allow someone to rob you. He will put that bat on you. He will shoot you. He will do whatever he has to do.
>
> *I:* How much respect is there for Frank out in the street?
>
> *Lee:* A hell of a lot. Even though people don't like to respect him, they don't have no choice.

> *Paul:* I seen him hit Brandon in the head. I seen him hit women and men with a baseball bat. They call it Batman's Place. I mean, he whips ass. He don't allow no fights and no pot-smoking. It ain't nothing but a hole in the wall. If you get caught smoking pot, that's a fight with him. If you get caught drinking and you did not buy it there, he's going to kick your ass. God forbid, don't ever fight in there. He's sharp—he shot Mark, and he shot Greg. But he gave them a chance to leave. He told them to leave and they didn't leave, so he just busted a cap in their ass.
>
> *I:* He told me that he even went to Mark's mother and asked her to please come and get her son. She wouldn't come. She said she couldn't do nothing with him.
>
> *Paul:* So he popped a cap in his ass. He's that kind of person, if he tell you to leave, leave.

A respondent who was also a law enforcement officer corroborated other respondents' descriptions of Frank's as the most violent black bar in the city. He also believed that the extended hours and the type of clientele the setting attracts combined to make it the most dangerous bar in the neighborhood:

> *I:* Which of the black bars do you consider prone to have the most violent confrontations?
>
> *Walker:* I'd say Frank's would be about number one.

> *I:* What is it about the people who go to Frank's that causes it to be the number-one bar involving violence?
>
> *Walker:* The people that frequent Frank's the most are younger, unemployed, the not so well educated. Second would be people who hang out after two o'clock; you got a mixture. That kind of mixture never works, and it causes violence.

Frank operated an illegal bar that was often the scene of violent confrontations, yet the police allowed the establishment to operate. I asked the respondent who was a law-enforcement officer why the police had not attempted to close Frank's down:

> *Walker:* Frank is just a person with a little bit of education that has a mind for making money. He bends the rules a little bit. The white cops don't bother him because Frank more or less takes care of his own. He takes care of the people up there. If there is a white person that comes in there for a drink and somebody's gonna rob them, Frank pulls his gun or his bat out. He won't have that up there at his place, which is wrong, but white cops figure, "Hey, if he can handle it, we don't have to go up there and take a chance about getting hurt." Frank's been taking care of that corner for a long time. He has shot and beat many people.
>
> *I:* Why do local law enforcement tolerate Frank's operating sort of as a bar?
>
> *Walker:* They sell illegal liquor. After two A.M. you got wall-to-wall brothers up there, and on the night shift you don't have that many cops working. If there is an altercation up there, the wave is small. You can't go up there with no small wave and make out because the brothers will hurt you. That's one reason why Frank gets away with a lot of stuff. I get along great with Frank. I don't have the problems they have. Frank takes care of his own. Frank shoots on the average three or four people a year. Frank don't do no time. Frank ain't went to jail yet. Frank shot three people in one night. He will beat your brains out with a bat. He'll go to jail for the weekend, and that's it.

When I interviewed Frank, I asked him to describe a typical set of circumstances that would lead him to use violence against a customer. He provided the following account:

> *Frank:* When I'm trying to get them out of my place, I do what I got to do. If I got to kill one, I'll do it.
>
> *I:* To keep your place running smoothly?
>
> *Frank:* That's right.

I: So a lot of times when something happens, it's because people won't listen to your rules?

Frank: Yeah. They come behind my counter, I'll stop them. I'll do anything I can. You would too.

I: Some people say it is dangerous to come up to Frank's because of the different kind of people that hang out there. Do you think that's true?

Frank: No, it's not. Anywhere you go is dangerous. You can get into it anywhere you go. It's how you carry yourself.

Conclusion

The primary purpose of this chapter has been to describe how black men interpret and define routine activities related to frequenting bars and bar settings. The impression recorded above suggest that black men who spend an inordinate amount of time in bars and bar settings have internalized a great many definitions of the social functions of these settings for themselves. The respondents hypothesized, for example, that they and their peers frequented black bars and bar settings for several reasons, including to socialize with their relatives and friends, to buy, sell or consume drugs, to initiate heterosexual relationships, and to manipulate and exploit others.

In addition, the respondents defined the black bars and bar settings frequented by lower-class blacks as fateful social settings. This definition was related to a shared understanding that these settings were often the location of acts of interpersonal behavior that are consequential and possess reputational implications.

In addition, the belief that most black men who frequent lower-class black bars and bar settings carry weapons and are willing to use those weapons against each other contributed to the perception of bars and bar settings as fateful environments within the black community.

The observations of the respondents suggest that black men are aware of rules of conduct that exist to regulate their behavior when they enter bars and bar settings. There were two rules that the respondents cited and discussed: "Mind your own business," and "Avoid trouble."

In addition to these two rules, it may be justified to include "Don't disrespect others" as a third. Many respondents, however, associated disrespecting others with violations of the "Avoid trouble" rule. Furthermore, when I asked respondents to list and describe major factors contributing to violent confrontations between black men, disrespect was listed more often as a cause of violence than as a rule violation. The perception of disrespect as a major cause of violence is substantiated by the responses summarized in Chapter 7. In reminiscing about precipitating events leading to their confrontations, the respondents cited demonstrations of disrespect toward them by their antagonists as a major cause of conflict.

Finally, the respondents indicated that they were very aware that black bars and bar settings are often the location of violent confrontations. When asked to describe the major factors contributing to violent confrontations between black men, they listed drug disputes; women, romantic competition, and jealousy; unemployment and economic jealousy; disrespect; and alcohol intoxication.

I now turn to interview responses related to the structure and interpersonal dynamics of violent confrontations in which the respondents were involved.

7

THE VIOLENCE PROCESS

The following discussion of the sequence of events and interpersonal processes associated with violent confrontations between black men is based on respondents' accounts of 86 violent confrontations and 30 incidents involving arguments that respondents perceived as potentially violent. The distribution of incident type is shown in Table 7–1.

Precipitating Events and Definition of the Situation

The first stage in the sequence of events leading to interpersonal violence is often referred to as the precipitating event. The term *precipitating event* is used here to refer to verbal statements, nonverbal behavior, and/or other actions that induce anger and an awareness that interpersonal violence is a possible consequence of a particular encounter. Thus, a precipitating event is behavior that is distinct from other behavior in that it is defined as having violence potential.[1]

Analysis of the accounts that the respondents provided suggests that three distinguishable types of precipitating events constituted the first stage of the violent confrontations in which the respondents were involved. The precipitating events they pointed to include loud talking and "getting bad," insults and identity attacks, and disrespect and unacceptable accounts.

80

Table 7–1
Respondents by Type of Incident

Respondent	Violent Confrontation	Potentially Violent Argument	Total Incidents
B. B.	0	2	2
Chast	1	1	2
Derrick	2	0	2
Terry B.	1	0	1
Big Bob	1	0	1
Brown	1	2	3
Dox	3	1	4
Turner	3	2	5
Houston	0	1	1
Rigsby	2	0	2
Mike	2	0	2
Hicks	3	2	5
Hawkins*	3	1	4
Harry B.	1	0	1
Patterson	3	1	4
Kessler	1	0	1
Don Juan	5	0	5
Cecil	1	0	1
Hendricks	1	1	2
Lender	1	1	2
Frank*	4	0	4
Ozell	4	1	5
Juan W.	3	1	4
Johnny B.	1	2	3
Germ	3	1	4
Lee	3	0	3
Willie B.	3	1	4
Paul	6	0	6
Holt	1	1	2
Troy	2	1	3
Mac	3	1	4
Lonzo	1	1	2
Walker	1	0	1
Butch	2	0	2
Watson	3	1	4
Joey	5	1	6
Washington	3	0	3
McKenzie	0	2	2
Carr	2	0	2
Sonny*	1	0	1
Jesse	3	1	4
Total 41	86	30	116

*These respondents were bar owners at the time the incidents they described occurred.

Loud Talking

For many of the incidents in which the respondents were involved, the pre-cipitating event they identified was a symbolic act. They cited, for example, subjective interpretations of the symbolic meanings of their antagonist's tone of voice, verbal comments, and/or nonverbal behavior as contributing to their definition of the situation in which violence was either anticipated or justified. Several respondents reported that they relied on their antagonist's tone of voice and verbal comments as indicators of their intentions.

The respondents used the term *loud talking* to refer to bellicose speech intended either to intimidate or to cast aspersions on the character of another individual. The definition of an antagonist's speech as loud talking was de-termined not only by the volume of the speech but by its content and forceful articulation in front of an audience. Several respondents reported that it is common for black men to loud-talk other men in order to promote them-selves at someone else's espense:

> *Patterson:* That's the way niggers are, man. They like to impress each other. If they feel there's a crowd around, they want to put on a show.

In situations in which the respondents believed that they were the target of loud talking, they generally attempted to mitigate the adverse effect of the statements. Their responses were motivated by concerns about their physical safety or reputation in the community:

> *Turner:* Too many people get off with the loud abusive talk.
> *I:* What does loud-talking someone do?
> *Turner:* The talk just keys somebody up. . . .
> *I:* What is it about talk that causes conflict?
> *Turner:* When you talk to somebody else aggressively, you automatically put them on the defense.
> *I:* Why do they go on the defensive?
> *Turner:* It's survival training.
> *I:* Do you think they feel threatened in some way?
> *Turner:* Of course. You have to feel threatened.
> *I:* Do they feel threatened from a physical standpoint, or do they also feel threatened from a social standpoint—I mean, do they feel threatened in terms of their reputation in the community?
> *Turner:* Both go hand in hand. At certain points, one always outweighs the other.

In the incident that is described below, the respondent and antagonist were friends. On several occasions prior to the violent encounter, however, the respondent had informed the antagonist that he was upset with him for telling his female friends that he was romantically involved with several of them. According to the respondent, "I told him once before to stay out of my business."

After the respondent and antagonist arrived at a bar along with three of their friends, the following events occurred:

> *Troy 2:*[*] See, when another female came to me to talk about it, "He told me this and all of this," you know. They did not want to say anything else to me. So I went to him and said, "Yo, I told you too many times about going to anybody that I am dealing with and talking to them about something you don't know about." So they come back to me. And if I am a man, I had to have a talk with him.
>
> *I:* Did you talk to him in a normal tone of voice?
>
> *Troy 2:* Yes. I tried, brother, I tried talking to him.
>
> *I:* What did he say to you?
>
> *Troy 2:* He wanted to get bad.
>
> *I:* How did he get bad?
>
> *Troy 2:* He came out of his mouth wrong.
>
> *I:* What did he say?
>
> *Troy 2:* "Fuck you!" If you are going to hang with me, don't buy that to me. What's between me and you is between me and you and nobody else.
>
> *I:* Did he say that in a loud voice?
>
> *Troy 2:* Yeah, the bar was packed. We were sitting there drinking, I'm spending the money, he ain't got no money.
>
> *I:* Was he trying to make you look bad?
>
> *Troy 2:* I don't care what anybody thinks about me, but if you are going to hang with me and help spend my money, we are going to get along. You don't want to get along, you step off. Don't be around me.
>
> *I:* After he got bad, what happened?
>
> *Troy 2:* We just fought.
>
> *I:* Who threw the first blow?
>
> *Troy 2:* I did.

Respondents felt compelled to respond to loud talking because they defined it as an attempt to cast aspersions on their manhood. A man who worked in one of the bars as a bouncer provided the following account:

---

[*]The number following a respondent's name represents a specific interview among a constellation of incidents in which data was collected from a particular respondent. In cases where a number does not follow a respondent's name, the quote is derived from interview responses that did not focus on a specific violent or potentially violent incident.

Watson 1: I was working, and a couple other people were throwing beers and stuff around the bar, and I had to go stop them. I don't know if they were fighting or not, but other people were getting wet by the beer and they were getting upset, so they called me over and I tried to talk to the man—telling him to stop... I asked him, would he please stop throwing the beer, or he would have to leave the bar. Then he started running his mouth.

I: What does that mean?

Watson 1: In other words, he was speaking words that were not necessary.

I: What kind of words? When he started talking to you, the main point that he was trying to communicate to you was what? And the main point that you were trying to communicate to him was what?

Watson 1: The main point he was communicating to me was like he was getting upset and wanted a little violence.

I: That's what he said?

Watson 1: That's what he wanted.

I: Is that what he said?

Watson 1: You might as well say that's what he said.

I: What did he say?

Watson 1: "Get the fuck out of my face, or I'll bust your ass." In other words, he was telling me what he wanted to do.

I: And what was the main thing you were saying back to him?

Watson 1: "Just cool off, just chill out, if not, I had to go call the cops."... I was doing my job. He made me feel that I should retaliate. I should have jumped on him.

I: Why should you have jumped on him?

Watson 1: Because he was taking away what little pride I have—not pride—but what little respect I do have.

I: What does that mean? I don't quite understand that.

Watson 1: In other words, by him saying what he said in front of all these people, it's just making me punk down.

The examples of loud talking that were cited above suggest that loud talking is a mode of communication in which black men direct challenges, insults, hostile rejoinder, and threats at one another.

In incidents precipitated by loud talking, the respondents reported that they often responded to their antagonists with loud talk. Loud-talking someone was also used to communicate overt and symbolic messages about oneself to third parties who were present to witness an incident between a respondent and an antagonist.

In the incident described below, which took place in 1971, the respondent (Turner 1) verbally threatened to assault the antagonist after the antagonist accidentally knocked over his beer. Several patrons and the bar owner attempted to mediate the situation by offering to buy the respondent another beer. Finally, the bar owner gave the respondent another beer. The respondent claimed that he was not totally satisfied with this solution, however, because he had wanted the antagonist to pay for the beer. According to the respondent, his overt reaction to the accidental action of the antagonist was influenced by the presence of two men with whom he had argued previously:

> *I:* What was unique about them being present?
>
> *Turner 1:* It called for a little extra loudness and a little more showboat.
>
> *I:* What does that mean? What were you trying to do?
>
> *Turner 1:* I'm actually provoking him to a certain extent.
>
> *I:* Provoking him to do what?
>
> *Turner 1:* To attack me.
>
> *I:* In order to do what?
>
> *Turner 1:* So I can dust him off. To impress the other guys that this is what you've got coming. If you transgress. If you bullshit and you mess around and you step on my space, then this is what you've got coming.
>
> *I:* Were you aware of them observing the situation?
>
> *Turner 1:* Oh, yeah. I wanted them to be aware of my potential. . . . To do damage, to hurt somebody.
>
> *I:* Why did you want them to know that?
>
> *Turner 1:* It's to keep them off me. To provide more space for myself.
>
> *I:* What had happened to make you think that these people might want to do some damage to you?
>
> *Turner 1:* I had already been in a fight with one of them, and I had been in an altercation with another one.
>
> *I:* Did their presence influence your behavior?
>
> *Turner 1:* To a certain extent, yes. I got an opportunity to more or less present my wares.
>
> *I:* What wares?
>
> *Turner 1:* The violence. Violence was my stock in trade then. It was the only thing I did good. I didn't work. I didn't do anything else besides hustle and shit. But fighting was what I did best. It was what I liked to do the most. That's what I enjoyed doing more than anything else.

This respondent reported that he deliberately loud-talked the antagonist in order to promote a tough guy image and to establish a reputation for violence. At the time when this incident occurred, this respondent was twenty-one years old and had lived in the city for only three months and, therefore, did not have a reputation in the community. His actions were to a certain extent motivated by a basic understanding that men who possess "tough guy" reputations are generally left alone. The following statements by respondents who were thirty-four and thirty-seven years of age when I interviewed them describe the protective significance of a "tough guy" reputation:

Paul: I live off my old reputation.

I: What does that mean?

Paul: When I was a lot younger, I didn't take no shit. A lot of people know me and they give me that leeway. They know I will hurt them, so they stay off me.

I: Do you think that your rep keeps people off your ass?

Brown: Yeah. Because when I was young I raised a lot of hell like everybody else did. I didn't take no wooden nickels. I'd fight every day and do a little bit of this, do a little bit of that.

After the respondent (Turner 1) and the antagonist who had accidentally knocked over his beer left the bar, the following events occurred, resulting in the death of the antagonist:

Turner 1: So maybe thirty or forty minutes later we leave. We go outside, he walks to the right and to the big building on West Street on the corner here. He goes that way, I go to the left. I live right here on this street, and I was coming down this way. When I got to the corner of Miller Street, I ran into a friend of mine. So me and him sit at this end and rap. At the time I was smoking Marlboros. I had the box in my shirt pocket. I gave him a cigarette, I took one, and there wasn't any more in the box, and instead of throwing the box away, I put the box in my shirt pocket. This guy that I had just got in the argument with walks up and asks me for a cigarette. I told him, "Man, I ain't got no more." He said, "You're a goddamn liar. You just put the pack back in your pocket." I just went off on him. I said, "I don't give a fuck what I put in my pocket, it ain't none of your goddamn business. If I did have some, you ain't getting none." It just happened that he took another step toward me. I just happened to see something flash in his hand. He had a knife in his hand, but I didn't think it would come off like that. It had to be something to make him blow up like that. He took a step toward me, and after that everything just went blank.

> *I:* What do you mean, everything went blank?
> *Turner 1:* I don't remember the exact sequence of what happened. It's like something just took over.
> *I:* So he asks you for a cigarette, you say you don't have a cigarette, he starts toward you, you see something flash—
> *Turner 1:* And after that I just went off. I went off on him physically. I wound up taking the knife from him and stabbing him with it.
> *I:* How many times did you stab him?
> *Turner 1:* Three times.
> *I:* Where?
> *Turner 1:* Two in the stomach and once in the side.
> *I:* Why did you stab him?
> *Turner 1:* I don't have an explanation for why I stabbed him. I just went on autopilot. I don't remember nothing. At that time, I just had come back from Vietnam. I was in that combat mode.

In 1986, fifteen years after he had murdered this man and had been involved in numerous other fights, the same respondent was involved in a violent confrontation with a man who had been drinking and driving and subsequently crashed into the respondent's new car. The car was parked in front of an after-hours joint. Unlike in 1971, when he had been a newcomer to the city, the respondent now knew that the people witnessing the confrontation between him and this antagonist were aware of his proficiency in violence. He had established a reputation:

> *Turner 5:* I have a reputation for hurting people.
> *I:* What does that mean?
> *Turner 5:* If you bother me, you cause a little more hell than you bargained for. You could get hurt. You could get cut, you could get shot.

Unlike the first incident (Turner 1), in this incident the respondent (Turner 5) claims that he did not want to fight his antagonist because he did not feel compelled to prove anything to anyone. However, after the antagonist refused to cooperate with his attempts to determine what happened to his car and threw a punch at him, the respondent reports that he responded with violence: he knocked the antagonist down on the ground at least five times. According to the respondent, he resorted to violence to protect himself. Each time he knocked the antagonist down, the antagonist got back up and attempted to attack the respondent. After five knock-downs, the incident was terminated when the police arrived in response to the respondent's call to investigate the damage to his car.

"Getting Bad"

In addition to loud-talking someone, certain nonverbal behaviors that attribute "getting bad" meanings increase the likelihood that an argument will escalate and result in a violent confrontation. The respondents used the term *getting bad* to characterize how an antagonist might attempt to intimidate and force them to back down from asserting a claim against the antagonist and/or demanding that the antagonist provide an acceptable justification for committing an act of wrongdoing against the respondent or a relative or friend of the respondent. Specific indicators of "getting bad" include loud talking, expressing open defiance, and displaying an unwillingness to negotiate conflict in a civil manner. The respondents were very aware of how verbal and nonverbal behavior could be employed and interpreted to signal an individual's intent in a conflict-ridden situation:

> *Washington 1:* Actually, I looked at him like, you know, what in the hell is he talking about. But I think that's why I never stood up. I felt like if I had stood up, that may have caused a greater problem. That's one of the reasons why I continued to sit down when I was talking to him.
>
> *I:* What were you saying to him?
>
> *Washington 1:* I was trying to get him to see my point of view . . . to get him to leave me alone.
>
> *I:* If you had stood up, that would have said what?
>
> *Washington 1:* I think that would have made it look like I wanted to fight him. I was actually trying to avoid a confrontation. If I would have stood up, I think that would have been like a sign of intimidation.

Sometimes playful aggression—pushing and shoving—can symbolically test the waters, to ascertain whether a conflict is serious or is susceptible to reconciliation. In the incident described below, the antagonist and a friend stole a check and gave it to the respondent to cash. The respondent cashed the check but decided he would keep all the money for himself:

> *Willie B. 1:* They came to me to cash the check. Both of these niggers knew enough about cashing stolen checks. So I said to myself, "Why did they come to me? They must want me to get caught." I cashed the check. But when I cashed it . . . I didn't give either of them no money. I kept the money for myself because I figured that I took the chance. I could have went to jail.

Subsequently, one of the men who stole the check periodically reminded the respondent when he saw him in a bar or on a street corner that he owed him money and he wanted to be paid. On one occasion, the respondent and his antagonist engaged in some partially serious banter and play boxing in which, although the respondent refrained from hitting the antagonist, he claims that the antagonist was making an effort to hit him. According to the respondent, he refrained from hitting the antagonist because he wanted to avoid escalating the conflict into a full-blown violent confrontation:

Willie B. 1: I was walking up there in front of the Galaxy, and I seen Hicks. So he started that same old stuff again.

    I: What did he say to you?

Willie B. 1: He said, "You got my money?" I said, "What money? I don't owe you no money." He started to try to throw his hands up. So I said, "I ain't running." So I threw my hands up, and we started boxing. He couldn't hit me. I could have hit him a lot of times.

    I: Why didn't you hit him?

Willie B. 1: I didn't want it to get serious.

    I: If you had hit him, that would have made it serious?

Willie B. 1: Yeah, I didn't want it to get serious.

    I: How did it end?

Willie B. 1: He said, "Billy, you pay me my money." Then he walked away.

    I: What did you think of that?

Willie B. 1: I said, "This nigger's showing off again." So then when I was walking down the street, this lady said something to him. And he said, "Yeah, that motherfucker," and he picked up a chair and threw it at me.

Insults and Identity Attacks

The term *insult* is generally defined as a statement or action that hurts or is meant to hurt another individual. Insults are often used to cast aspersions on an individual's character. Consequently, insults pose a threat to identity and self-perceptions. Loud talking, "getting bad," insults, and identity attacks are not mutually exclusive as precipitating events or forms of violence-provoking behavior. However, they are distinct in terms of how black men attribute meaning to them. The salient meanings that they commonly attribute to loud talking and "getting bad," for example, relate to their concerns with avoiding attempts by an antagonist to publicly intimidate and/or successfully violate their autonomy in a socially important public setting. Insults and identity attacks, by contrast, are perceived as potentially threatening to their self-image. Therefore, responses to insults and identity attacks primarily emerge not out of a desire to impress others in the setting but out of a desire to protect and preserve a positive image of one's self for one's self.

Violent confrontations that occur among black males in bars and bar settings are often precipitated by an insult. The men I interviewed were particularly sensitive to insults that they defined as casting aspersions on their manhood. To be called a punk was regarded as the ultimate insult. Moreover, the punk insult was more likely than other insults to lead an encounter toward a violent conclusion:

> *Houston:* The word *faggot* or something like that is used to take your manhood away.
>
> *I:* Why do you think that so many fights among black males are centered around manhood?
>
> *Houston:* I believe with us, the black man, that our manhood is very important to us. That's about the only thing we have to hold on to—besides our families—is our manhood. And when that's threatened, it's time to fight. "I'm going to show you that I'm not a punk," "I'm going to show you that I'm not a faggot"—you know, that sort of thing. I've seen fights where words were exchanged for at least ten, fifteen minutes and they just stood there and exchanged words with one another, and one guy told the other guy, "Look, just leave me alone," and the other guy just kept on you know, "Fuck you punk," and the other guy was getting tired of the exchange of words, being called punk, faggot, sissy, so forth, that he just went on ahead and punched the guy, and a fight occurred.
>
> *I:* What would you say is the most important factor contributing to fights between black males?
>
> *Houston:* Manhood—you know, a challenge to their manhood.

The incident described below conforms completely with this respondent's account of how insults lead to interpersonal violence among black men. In this incident, the respondent (Dox 2), the antagonist and three women were sitting in an after-hours joint around noontime. The antagonist had bought a bottle of wine; one of the women opened it and poured everyone a serving, including the respondent. The antagonist did not invite the respondent to drink any of his wine.

According to the respondent, the antagonist initiated the confrontation by loud-talking him. The antagonist accused the respondent of preferring to beat up women rather than fight a man. They argued for over an hour.

The respondent indicated that before the incident he was already aware that the antagonist did not like him. He believed that the antagonist was jealous of his success with women:

> *Dox 2:* Because to look at him and to look at me, you see why he was acting like that.

I: What's the difference?

Dox 2: Well, he look like he's about forty-two years old, he gotta pay for all the women he be with, and I don't have to do that. So I feel like all this is building up. See, all this is building up to the point where . . . you know he was jealous. So he calls me all these names . . . . He called me about eight bitches.

I: He called you a bitch?

Dox 2: Yeah, and about seven faggots.

I: Was he loud?

Dox 2: Real loud! He was talking about I only wanted trouble. I'm gonna get in some trouble with a woman. I'm not gonna fight with no man. . . . Well, he was calling me out of my name. But I tried to ignore that, but it had got to the point where I couldn't. He said that he was thinking about whipping my ass.

I: When he said that, what happened?

Dox 2: I gave him a real hard left.

I: Why was it necessary to give him a real hard left-hand at that point?

Dox 2: Because he was threatening me, and I felt like if I don't do it now . . . I was going to have to see him later, that he was going do it again and I wanted to leave earlier. It was like he had me up against the wall. And I felt like, if I didn't do him, he was going to do me. See, so it was a matter of self-preservation. It wasn't like I was looking for trouble.

I: After you hit him, what happened then?

Dox 2: Well, he dropped. I put my foot right in his face because I felt like if he got up, he's going to be real mad. But he didn't get up. So they called the ambulance and I left. The police picked me up two blocks away . . . took me downtown and when I told the police that it was self-defense—and what would you do—they gave me an appearance ticket.

This incident suggests that a man's decision to use violence against another man may be influenced by several factors. In this incident, for example, the respondent claims that he hit the antagonist because he thought that the antagonist was about to physically assault him. Later on in the interview, however, the respondent restates the view that the insults directed against him by the antagonist constituted an attack on his manhood and that this was too much for him to accept:

Dox 2: He called a man bitches, punks, and faggots. And a man can only take so much. He tried to take my manhood. I mean, he was taking my manhood. How many bitches and faggots can I be?

Defining a statement or action as questioning or challenging one's manhood may lead to violent confrontations even between friends. In the incident described below, the respondent, age thirty-five, and the antagonist, age twenty-four, at the time of the incident, were both attending a truck-driving school. The respondent saw himself as playing a big brother role in the relationship. He had encouraged the antagonist to not drop out of school after he received his financial aid grant. The respondent also indicated that he and the antagonist competed against each other in school. On the day the incident occured, they had stopped by one of the after-hours joints to have a beer after school:

Mac 3: Me and Jeff had a few beers, and we got on the kick about who could out-drive who. "I can out-drive you, and you can't out-drive me.". . . So at that point I said, "Oh, man, you're getting serious." He said, "Yeah, man, I'm getting serious." I said, "I knew you, man, when you were running around with your nose snotty," and I shouldn't have said that.

I: Were people already listening to the conversation?

Mac 3: Yeah, they're listening, they're enjoying us.

I: So you all are having fun?

Mac 3: Yeah, right. We were actually having fun, but it changed when I said, "I remember when you was running around with your nose snotty, and I use to wipe your nose." And I shouldn't have never said that.

I: When you said that, what did he say?

Mac 3: He said, "I'm a man. I'll kick your motherfucking ass." I said, "Now wait a minute, Jeff, I'm not taking any ass-whipping." He says, "I'm a man, too. I'll kick your motherfucking ass right now!" I says, "Well hold up, Jeff. I tell you what, you don't say nothing to me no more, I won't say nothing to you. Okay, we'll squash this shit then." He says, "We ain't got to squash nothing, we can go outside." Now everybody's up here hearing this stuff.

I: How do you feel about what he's saying?

Mac 3: Well, I feel that he feels that he's a man, but I really don't want to fight him because the family is too tight, too close. . . . But the guy's not going to let me out the place unless I fight him now. He actually stood in front of the door and wouldn't let me go out. He said, "You gonna fight me?" So now I'm saying, "Jeff, I don't want to fight you, man." But he is saying, "I'm going to kick your ass, kick you this, kick you that." I said, "Okay, Jeff, if that's what you want, okay." I takes off my coat, walks outside, he takes off his, we go outside, and then we blow. Boom, boom, boom. I pop him a couple good times. By this time I'm feeling sorry, I don't want to do this. Now it's done changed now. Now he's reaching in his pocket like he's got a knife. Actually, he's trying to get me off of him. He's faking, but I ain't taking no chances. I leave the scene.

I: You left?

Mac 3: Yeah, I leave the scene. I left fast. Now he's running at me. So I'm backing off, I'm getting away from him. Now he stops running, and he starts running towards his house. So now I'm figuring he ain't got nothing, so he's going to get his shotgun. Finally, a few days later, I'm up at Dee Dee's drinking a beer and really should have been watching my back. I had been talking to a few guys about it, they heard about it. Instead of watching my back, I've got my back to the door, he walks in and sneaks me.

I: With what, his fists?

Mac 3: Yeah, his fists. I got glasses on, he sneaks me and the glasses cut my eye. Then we scuffled in Dee Dee's for a while. They break it up, and he walks out. Now I'm begging him to come on, come on back. After he sneaks me and they break it up, he took off.

Disrespect and Unacceptable Accounts

Insults disrupt the normative order that regulates interpersonal relations. To reestablish normative order, individuals who have violated rules of conduct will often offer excuses or justifications in order to explain their actions and to apologize to those they have offended. Lyman and Scott have introduced the term *account* to describe this process. They use the term account to refer to "a statement made by a social actor to explain unanticipated or untoward behavior."[1]

The primary purpose of providing an account—that is, an excuse or justification—is to restore balance in a relationship that one of the participants has disrupted by violating expected rules of conduct. Stokes and Hewitt use the term *alignment* to refer to the same interpersonal process. However, whereas Lyman and Scott emphasize verbal statements that people offer to explain behavior that they or someone else defines as inappropriate or unacceptable, Stokes and Hewitt attempt to demonstrate how both alignment and misalignment of interpersonal relations are influenced by cultural values, norms, and definitions of the situation.

According to Stokes and Hewitt, when interpersonal relations are disrupted or misaligned, individuals often seek to restore normative order by realigning themselves. Thus the term *alignment* is used to refer:

(1) a mutual orientation of conduct . . . by participants to align their individual acts, one to another, in the creation of joint or social acts; and (2)

perceived discrepancies between what is actually taking place in a given situation and what is thought to be typical, normatively expected, probable, desirable or, in other respects, more in accord with what is culturally normal.[3]

Consequently, when individuals are perceived as having violated rules of conduct and fail to offer an account or pursue a line of action that leads toward realignment, the likelihood that interpersonal conflict will escalate toward a violent confrontation increases.

The most common precipitating event that respondents mentioned involved situations in which the respondent had either directly observed or was informed by a relative or friend that an antagonist had committed an unacceptable act against them. The respondent initiated contact with the antagonist by requesting that he provide an account of his behavior. Violence tended to occur when the respondent defined the antagonist's response to his request for an account, or his efforts to effect alignment, as disrespectful and inappropriate.

Two months prior to a violent confrontation between one respondent (Chast) and an antagonist, they had engaged in a serious argument that the respondent defined as potentially violent. In that situation, the respondent had walked into a bar and immediately observed that the antagonist was harassing his girlfriend, who was working as a bartender. The respondent informed the antagonist that the bartender was his girlfriend and that he did not appreciate how the antagonist was speaking to her. Violence was avoided because the antagonist apologized:

Chast 1: He said, "These guys didn't tell me anything, I was just talking to the lady."

I: Did you feel satisfied that he gave you an appropriate apology at that time?

Chast 1: Yes. And I apologized to him. I was kind of harsh with him, I would say. I was just as hard, I think, as he was with my old lady. I cussed him because he cussed her.

I: Why did you apologize to him?

Chast 1: He didn't know she was my lady. Certain people are like he is—they act and they don't think.

I: So you gave him the benefit of the doubt. If he had known that was your woman, he wouldn't have treated her like that?

Chast 1: Yes.

Two months later, however, the respondent (Chast) was at home when a friend came by and reported that the antagonist was at the bar swearing at his girlfriend and refusing to pay his bar bill. Subsequently, the respondent went to the bar to confront the antagonist:

Chast 2: I was trying to tell him that what he was doing was wrong and that it was embarrassing to the woman. And it was embarrassing to me. . . .

I: Why was it embarrassing to you?

Chast 2: Anybody that talks or swears at anybody related to me is embarrassing to me. It was more embarrassing for her, I would think. It was very insulting to me because I had mentioned it to him before.

I: When you were talking to him, was he trying to say or tell you anything?

Chast 2: He was trying to make a point to me that he didn't care what my thoughts was, and what he was doing was correct for him.

I: What did he say to give you that impression?

Chast 2: He said, "Fuck you and your woman," after I told him what I thought was his fault. We didn't do too much talking after that. After he said that, I decked him.

I: Why did you hit him?

Chast 2: I had enough of trying to reason with him, and that was it. He showed me a total lack of respect. This is one of the main reasons why I hit him.

Attempts to restore normative order after an antagonist disrupts interpersonal relations by committing a rule violation against a relative or friend may lead to a violent confrontation between the antagonist and the individual who intervenes to defend his relative or friend against insult or physical injury. While the individual who intervenes is initially motivated to intervene out of a sense of loyalty and a desire to defend the relative or friend, however, the antagonist's unacceptable response to the intervener's request for an account leads the intervener to personalize the statements or actions of the antagonist. Disrespectful responses to requests for an account or efforts to align disrupted relations may lead the intervener to define the antagonist's statements and actions as not only directed against his relative or friend but against himself. Thus, in violent confrontations in which an individual intervenes in a situation to defend a relative or friend, violence tends to occur after the intervener personalizes the statements and/or actions of the antagonist:

Turner 4: My brother was drunk one day, and some dude was fucking with him. When I drive up, the dude is standing there with his finger in his face, pointing at him and shit. So I get out of the car and say, "Yo man, what the fuck's up?" He said, "Man, this motherfucker here." I said, "Yo, man, check it out, that's my brother you're talking to man." He said, "I don't give a fuck if it's your mammy." When he said that, I capped him.

I: Why did you hit him?

Turner 4: Because when he said, "I wouldn't give a damn if it was your mammy," he done already let me know what's on his mind. He got doing something to my brother on his mind, and I don't seem to faze him at all.

I: How come you didn't just walk away?

Turner 4: Because he didn't give me no opportunity to walk away. Coming out of his mouth like that just let me know that he had no respect for me or mine or nothing else.

I: So what were you trying to achieve by hitting him?

Turner 4: Letting him know that this ain't gonna get it, man. You got to respect something in life, and my mother's going be one of them.

Lee 1: There was this brother who was from out of town, and he was partying in Ann's World, and he kept bugging my woman and my sister. And they asked me to ask the brother to cut them some slack.

I: How was he bugging them?

Lee 1: Talking to them and trying to rap to them. Trying to make plays for them, and they weren't interested, and they didn't want to hear it. They told him they had old men and he didn't acknowledge that. So they asked me to speak to him. So I spoke to the brother and told him that "this is my woman and this is my sister and I would appreciate it if you didn't bother them." And then he disrespected me. He said, "What the fuck you got to do with it? What do you want to do?" So I told the brother, "let's go outside." So he came outside, and the fight was on.

I: Why did you ask him to go outside?

Lee 1: Because he got loud and totally disrespected me. That's why I asked him to go outside. I was mad, and I was ready to fight then.

Loud-talking someone is an unacceptable response to a request for an account of one's behavior or efforts to align disrupted relations. Moreover, this type of response enhances the likelihood that violence will occur because the respondent interprets the antagonist's verbal statements as a personal insult and a sign that he is unwilling to enter into dialogue oriented toward nonviolent closure of the encounter:

I: When he got loud with you, what was the main point he was trying to communicate to you?

Lee 1: He was chumping me off. He was putting me in a position where he was telling me I didn't have no right to be there for my sister, my woman, or myself.

I: So when you got outside, what happened?

Lee 1: We commenced to fighting.

I: Did he violate any rules of behavior?

Lee 1: When he loud-talked me, he totally disrespected me. He was through, then . . . that was a fight then. There was no way he could get around it.

I: Why was that crossing the line? Why was that the straw that broke the camel's back?

Lee 1: Young black men, here and a lot of other places that I have been, we just don't accept being disrespected. Not only by our friends and family but especially by strangers.

In several incidents, including the above, the transition from dialogue to violence occurred very rapidly after an antagonist provided an unacceptable account. The following is another illustration:

Paul 1: A female friend of mine and I were out partying and having a pretty good time. Then this fellow comes up to her and said, "I'm going to fuck you when I get a chance. And, if you won't give me none, I am going to kick your ass and rape you." So I said, "Yo man, this is my cousin." And he says, "Well, I don't give a fuck." So I popped him upside his head with a bottle of Miller beer.

I: Why did you hit him?

Paul 1: He disrespected me.

I: What happened then?

Paul 1: I must have put my foot on him until we were pulled apart, and they took him outside.

Individuals who either observed or were informed by others that a relative or friend had been insulted or physically assaulted tended to anticipate a violent resolution of the conflict with the antagonist.

In most of the incidents precipitated by an offense committed against a relative or friend, the individual who intervened requested an account or attempted to align relations that had been disrupted. Violence tended to occur after the antagonist provided an account that the intervenor defined as unacceptable. In a few incidents, however, the intervenor was not interested in hearing an account or attempting to bring about a nonviolent alignment of disrupted relations. In situations of this type the intervenor initiated violence against the antagonist immediately upon coming into personal contact with him:

Chast 2: I came down there to get this dude straight, whether he was going to kick my ass or not. I had intentions of punching him out. . . . There was nothing he could apologize for anymore.

> *Germ 3:* He didn't give me a chance to tell him what happened, at all. He didn't let me explain myself, he just started swinging at me.

Third Parties

All of the violent confrontations that the respondents described occurred in the presence of third parties. This finding is largely a result of the decision to limit the focus of the study to violent confrontations that occurred in bars and bar settings. Consequently, given the centrality of bars and bar settings in facilitating sociability among lower-class blacks, it is inevitable that violent confrontations in these settings would be witnessed by third parties.

Third parties exerted a significant effect on respondents' definitions of the situation, their decisions regarding the management of these encounters, and the structure and sequence of events leading to the deescalation or escalation of conflict.

Third parties were described by the respondents as assuming one of three roles in the arguments and violent confrontations in bars and bar settings. These roles include those of: mediators, instigators and instigating audience.

Mediators

Mediators were third parties who actively attempted to intervene in an encounter between a respondent and an antagonist to de-escalate conflict toward a nonviolent termination. Moreover, mediators tended to stand in a primary relationship, like friend or relative, to one or both of the participants:

> *Houston 1:* I went to go into the rest room, and this brother had his foot up against the door or whatever, and I kind of pushed the door, and I guess the door hit him or something like that. I walked in, and the brother turned around and looked at me and says, "Yo, man, you pushed the door on me!" Like that, and I say, "Hey, I'm sorry, excuse me. I didn't mean to, I didn't know you were behind the door." And then he got loud and said, "Look, man, I'll kick your motherfucking ass. I'll kick your ass right here, right now." So I just looked at the brother and I told the brother, "Look, why don't you just calm down. Why don't you just chill out. I already apologized to you about the situation, I don't think that's necessary." So then he was saying, "I'll kick your ass." So I said, "Hey man, I think you should calm down." So my friend turned and said, "Look, man, this is a friend of mine . . . he's

okay, just chill out." He told the other guy, "Look, he's one of my people, don't worry about it."

Chast 2: A couple of guys I knew, they knew what was going on. They came toward me and just said it wasn't worth it, it doesn't matter.

Mediation was often unsuccessful in situations in which only one of the participants was being subjected to third-party intervention:

Mac 1: I was in the bar with my wife, and somebody came up to me and said, "Your brother is in a fight." So I left the bar and went down to the corner . . . and there was a big crowd, and my brother was involved in an argument. So I approached the scene and grabbed my brother. I said, "What's going on, man?" He says, "These two guys are trying to double-team me." So I tried to get him to leave with me, but they kept putting pressure on him.

I: How were they doing that?

Mac 1: By not leaving. When I was trying to get him away, they were following us around like they wanted something to happen, they wanted to fight. They were saying they were going to fuck him up.

I: What was your brother saying?

Mac 1: "One at a time, let's go."

I: What were you saying to your brother?

Mac 1: That it don't make no sense because I knew that he had just got out of jail, and that's all he needed was to get in some trouble on State Street.

I: What happened next?

Mac 1: So one of the guys just insisted on fighting. At this point now I knew these guys were not leaving. They wanted to fight. So I let my brother go. I said, "As long as it's one on one, no problem." So they fought, they fought for a few minutes. I'd say about a good three minutes. We broke that up.

I: Who broke it up?

Mac 1: Me and a few other guys that were out in the street.

After the fight with the first antagonist was broken up, the respondent's brother shifted his attention to the second antagonist. The respondent's efforts to mediate the fight with the second antagonist also was met with resistance. In the second stage of this incident, however, the respondent reports that he experienced ambivalence about attempting to mediate the encounter after the second antagonist shot his brother:

Mac 1: This is where my brother was wrong. After he fought Jake, now he wants to fight the other one. Instead of just leaving it at that and leaving, he wants to fight the other guy. He said, "Now it's your turn." Leo was scared to death. He had a brick in his hand. So while I'm trying to talk my brother into not fighting, somebody slips Leo a gun. He pointed it at us, you could see it in his eyes—he wanted to shoot both of us. . . . Now, I'm trying to sweet-talk this guy. "Yo, man, I'm up here trying to keep my brother from fighting. I'm trying to break this up."

I: What did Leo say?

Mac 1: He's looking at me like he wants to shoot me, but there's no reason to shoot me. . . .He shoots my brother in the leg. At this time I'm just about crazy now. Now I'm looking around for my relatives, which I'm glad I didn't see, because if someone gave me a gun, I would have shot him. I know I would be in jail right now. I would have shot him.

I: After he shot the weapon, what happened then?

Mac 1: Once he shot the weapon . . . it was so fast, my brother went and grabbed a brick, and the guy who shot him takes off. But the other guy was still there. My brother went to work on him with the brick and his fist. Now I'm thinking how can I stop him, when the guy's done shot him. I'd feel like an ass, but I had to do that because I didn't want him to kill the boy. So I did try to convince him to chill out, go to the hospital and see about his leg.

I: How could this situation have been prevented?

Mac 1: When I was getting my brother, somebody should have been getting Jake and Leo . . . talking to them. Then it could have been dispersed. I had my brother, but nobody is holding Jake and Leo. They were just standing there free.

Instigators

Instigators were third parties who assumed a proactive stance in violent incidents by provoking one participant to argue or fight with another participant. Unlike mediators, who generally intervened in a situation for the purpose of influencing one or both of the primary participants to terminate the display of hostility, instigators tended to direct their efforts toward provoking or inciting a participant to argue or fight.

The relationship between violent participants and third parties, particularly mediators and instigators, varied by the type of precipitating event that led to an interpersonal conflict. For example, in incidents precipitated by an antagonist against a relative or friend, those who were offended tended to encourage the respondent or intervener to argue or fight with the antagonist. In the section "Disrespect and Unacceptable Accounts," I provided a description of an incident in which the respondent had intervened and attempted to align relations between the antagonist and a female friend, after the antagonist said to the respondent's female friend: "I'm going to fuck you. And if you don't give me none, I'm going to kick your ass and rape you." Subsequently, the female friend supported the respondent's use of violence against the antagonist after his attempts to align the disrupted relations had failed:

> *I:* Did anyone encourage you to argue or fight with him?
> *Paul 1:* When I hit him, Sherry told me to kick his ass.

In another incident precipitated by defense of a relative, the respondent (Mac) was approached by the brother (Steve) of a man he had fought and beat a week earlier. In that incident, the respondent (Mac) claimed that the first brother/antagonist had violated the "mind your own business" rule by interfering in a conversation that the respondent was having, in which he was putting down the drug-dealer friends of the first brother/antagonist for selling the respondent's brother poor-quality drugs.

In the confrontation with the second/brother antagonist (Steve) the antagonist wanted to fight and beat up the respondent (Mac) for beating up his brother. The second brother/antagonist (Steve) was accompanied by a third brother/antagonist (Don Juan) who functioned as an instigator:

> *Mac 3:* His brother, Steve, come up to me and says that me and my brother jumped on his brother. He thought that we took advantage of his brother.
> *I:* Did you hear anyone encourage him to fight you?
> *Mac 3:* Yeah, his brother Don Juan was saying, "Kick his ass."

In incidents precipitated by loud talking and "getting bad" or insults and identity attacks, relatives and friends were more likely to intervene as mediators, while acquaintances and bystanders were more likely to instigate:

> *Willie B. 5:* I was standing in front of the Galaxy, and all of a sudden Hicks came up there and he started talking about, "You are going to give me my money. You are going to do this, or I'm going to get in your butt."
> *I:* Was he talking loud?
> *Willie B. 5:* Yeah, he was talking loud in front of everybody. Then he tried to kick me. That's when Hodge said, "Willie B., I know you ain't taking that junk from him. Get on him!"

The Instigating Audience

One of the major questions that I wanted to answer in the study was, How do face-saving or self-image-defending concerns influence decision-making in interpersonal transactions leading to violent confrontations between black males in bars and bar settings? Nearly all of the respondents reported that when the various incidents in which they were involved were unfolding, they were aware of "the crowd" observing them. Most of them, however, denied that their actions in the situation were motivated by a desire to look good in front of the crowd. According to most of the respondents, their primary concern was to avoid getting hurt:

> *Chast 2:* I was trying to fight, I wasn't concerned about looking good. I was trying to keep him off my ass and get into his ass.
> *I:* Did you want to look good?
> *Chast 2:* No, I was fighting. That's what you do when you fight. You fight. You try to keep the dude off your ass, and you try to get on his ass. You don't worry about looking good. You can talk about it afterwards if you get through it.

> *Mac 3:* I wasn't worried about anybody looking at me. I was worried about I knew I had been drinking and this guy is big, I just didn't want to get messed up . . . under the influence of alcohol.

While the respondent generally reported that their actions were not influenced by a desire to look good in front of the crowd, they frequently attributed this concern to their antagonists. Descriptions of how an antagonist was attempting to look good typically included references to the antagonist's use of loud talking, insults, and threats:

> *Chast 2:* I think he is always trying to look good. When we stopped fighting the first time, he was doing a lot of woofing. . . . He was telling me to come outside if I wanted to fight like a man.

> *I:* How do you know he was trying to embarrass you?
> *Houston 1:* From the loud tone of his voice and the way he acted when he put his finger in my face.

In addition to being concerned about what the antagonist was doing, some respondents reported that they surveyed the crowd to determine whether the antagonist had supporters present who would be willing to assist the antagonist:

Turner 5: I'm watching him, I'm in a physical thing now. I can't pay attention to the crowd now, but I got my eye on one person.

I: What one person?

Turner 5: One of his cousins.

I: What was the cousin doing?

Turner 5: Standing back watching.

While only two respondents admitted that they were trying to look good in front of the crowd, many expressed the view that they understood that it was important to act in a way that would deter others from attempting to take advantage of them in the future:

Willie B. 5: He was in my face. This kind of made me think that "I can't let this man treat me like this in front of all these people." That's the first thing I thought about.

This respondent also reported that failing to adequately respond to an antagonist could have negative ramifications in other areas of his life, including relations with women:

Willie B. 5: I don't want to look bad in front of other people. I don't want people picking on me. If they see him do it, then they want to do it. Then my life is ruined, because I won't have no respect from nobody. Everybody will be disrespecting me. Then I can't have a decent woman to bring out to the bar because they are going to be disrespecting me in front of the woman.

In addition to concerns about the importance of acting in a manner that will deter others from attempting to take advantage of them, face-saving and self-image-defending concerns were predominant in respondents' references to the instigating audience.

I use the term *instigating audience* to refer to bystanders who encouraged one or both participants in a conflict-ridden situation to resort to violence as a means of resolving interpersonal conflict. Unlike mediators and instigators, members of the instigating audience did not have a primary relationship with conflict participants. However, many respondents reported that bystanders who witnessed interpersonal conflict between black males in bars and bar settings were seldom innocent or neutral:

Hicks: You get feedback from the crowd. "Hey man, don't let that sucker chop you off like that." You know what I mean? Now this is motivating your anger. And you look and you want to walk away, but you got to prove to them that you are all man. And then you retaliate by verbally coming on or just physically assaulting this dude and letting him know, "Hey, man, I'll kick your ass" or whatever.

The same theme can be recognized in the following account:

Turner 4: Everybody wants me to do something.
     I: How do you know?
Turner 4: Because they all stood up in anticipation. They wanted somebody to fight. They don't want anybody to argue.
     I: Did anyone verbally say that?
Turner 4: No, but you can feel it. You can feel the tension. You can feel the excitement in the air. You look people in the face, and they are watching you. They are watching your reaction.

Several respondents expressed the view that the response of nonprimary third parties—bystanders—was influenced by collective evaluations of one or both of the participants. In the incident described below, the respondent and the antagonist were friends. However, when the respondent said to the antagonist, "I remember when you were running around with a snotty nose," the antagonist demanded that the respondent fight him:

> *Mac 3:* No, they were surprised because it ain't fun no more. . . . The people were saying, "Why are you all doing this? This don't make sense."

> *Washington 1:* Nobody intervened, nobody said anything. After he hit me and I fell on the floor and jumped back up and was getting ready to attack him, . . . that's when a couple of guys grabbed him, and one guy grabbed me and said it's not worth it. It wasn't worth fighting over a beer and that it was mine and I didn't have to share if I didn't want to. They were telling me there's no point in going any further with this.
>   *I:* Who were the guys who intervened?
> *Washington 1:* They were friends of both of ours.

In incidents in which one of the participants in an encounter was disliked by many of the bystanders, they urged the other participant to use violence against him:

> *Watson:* If it's somebody they can't stand, they want somebody to fight for them. That's why they want to see a fight. But if they both

be friends, they will stop them. If they don't like one of the people, they will let them go.

Chast 2: I was being held. I wanted to fight. . . . They let me go. He ran outside, and I came outside, and we fought for about twenty or thirty minutes.

I: Why did they let you go?

Chast 2: Most people that know Brandon don't like him. He knows it, and everybody that knows him knows it.

Some respondents felt that they were being manipulated and pushed into resorting to violence:

Turner: It's coming from people who don't have enough excitement in their own lives. They sit around and wait for something to happen to other people. They make it happen as much as possible. Oh, they love to see the spectacle.

Washington 2: It was like they were pouring gas on it.

I: How did you know they were doing that?

Washington 2: It's like they are encouraging you. Instead of them encouraging the argument to cease, they're encouraging it to continue. They want to see it escalate, they want to see it get larger instead of cooling the situation down. Instead of doing that, they do the opposite thing. They encourage, they push you together. It's like . . . as a matter of fact, at one point somebody said, "Well, why don't both of you all go outside to see who whips whose ass, and then we'll find out who was right and who was wrong."

Justifying Violence

The decision to use violence against another individual is a significant juncture of the violence process.[4] The men I interviewed tended to refer to one of four considerations that prompted them to resort to violence at the time. These contemporaneous justifications included rule violations, self-defense, alcohol intoxication, and violence as communication.

Disrespect: The Ultimate Rule Violation

In most of the incidents, excluding some of those precipitated by the antagonist initiating the physical assault, the decision to use violence against an individual was based on a definition of the antagonist's verbal statements and/or actions as being disrespectful:

Paul 1: If you go back to the first time when he told me to fuck you, I don't let anybody tell me to 'kiss my ass and fuck you.' I don't disrespect another man. I don't tell anyone to kiss my ass, and I ain't going to let anybody else tell me to kiss their ass.

References to disrespect as a good and sufficient reason to use violence against another individual were often associated with references to the belief that the antagonist's verbal statements and/or actions constituted a personal invasion or transgression against the respondent's autonomy:

Don Juan 1: I can only take so much. If I tell a person to leave me alone, leave me alone right then and there. But he pushed me to a point where I could just take so much. He's making me feel less than a man, by not leaving me alone when I asked him to. When he pushed me, he moushed me in my face. I don't go for that—nobody touches me.

Washington 1: I felt like he wasn't being courteous or respectful of my rights when I said no to him. But there's no written law that says he has to go along with what I think are my rights. But I think there's an unwritten thing about "I respect you, you respect me." It's respect. He disrespected me and my rights as a man. That right there alone made me mad, made me angry. Because he's refusing to see me as an individual and respect me as a person. And that's what really pissed me off. He was going to make me do something that I didn't want to do. I felt like he had a total disregard for my rights or my feelings or my being a human being in the first place. That's what causes a lot of problems.

Lee 3: Three weeks prior to the fight, me and my girlfriend were arguing a lot. And my friend would always come over and grab me and intervene in me and my girlfriend's argument. I asked him twice . . . "when me and my woman are arguing, stay out of my business, man. The next time you come over, me and you are going to have to fight." After a basketball game one night, me and my woman were arguing at Dee Dee's Lounge. He come over and interrupted. I had a drink in my hand, so I took my drink and I threw it in his face. So then me and him started wrestling. We knocked down a couple of tables. Then they broke us up.

I: Why did you throw the drink in his face?

Lee 3: Because as a man, what I say to him, tell him, or explain to him has no importance whatsoever. He totally disrespected me. I asked him not to do it, and I let him know prior to this that if he continued to do this we were going to fight. I just felt like he was totally disrespecting me as a friend, a partner, and a brother. And most of all, making me feel like I couldn't handle my own problems or my own life. It was my woman, not his. And it made me mad.

According to the respondent (Lee), this incident was precipitated by the antagonist when he violated the "mind your own business" rule. However, the respondent's intrapersonal decision to use violence was based purely on his definition of the antagonist's intervention in the argument as implying that he could not (or should not) handle his own affairs.

"Mind Your Own Business"

The men I interviewed generally attributed the cause of the violent confrontation between themselves and other men to some unacceptable statement or behavior directed against them, a relative, or friend by an antagonist. Exceptions to this trend were in accounts of incidents in which the "mind your own business" rule was violated. Several respondents reported that some of the incidents in which they were involved could have been avoided if they had personally honored the rule requiring men to mind their own business:

Don Juan 3: So this dude starts beating up this girl. And I tells him, "Why don't you take her home and do it." "It's none of your business," he says. "Forget it, she should bust your ass. . . ." That's what I said to him. So I walks away from him, I walks down the street. As I'm walking down the street, he started talking all this junk.

I: What did he say?

Don Juan 3: "Punk, motherfucker you should mind your business"— this and that. I says, "That's why I walked away from you. I ain't got nothing to do with it, go ahead. Your old lady's sisters got her now, so fuck it. Go on about your business." Now the cops are in it now. So the cops are standing right there in front of us. I said, "Officer, would you tell this dude to get out of my face." So he swung and hit me.

I: He hit you right in front of the cops?

Don Juan 3: Right in front of the cops. He didn't knock me out, though. I just staggered back a little bit. I looked at the cop, told the cop, "You saw him hit me." I hit him. I blasted him. They pulled me to the side, they were going to arrest me. But they didn't because he hit me first.

I: Why did he hit you?

Don Juan 3: I shouldn't have said nothing. I should have let him handle it his way.

Self-Defense

Respondents also saw their use of violence as justified by characterizing their actions as self-defense reactions to being threatened or assaulted by an antagonist. Unlike assaults, threats did not automatically move an encounter toward a violent confrontation. In incidents precipitated by threats, the decision to use violence against the antagonist was the result of influences from the antagonist's actions or the content of his speech and about his intent:

Dox 4: This guy started threatening me with a Thunderbird bottle. It was about a female. He asked me why I was at her house. I said, yes, I had been at her house. I think he might have saw me coming from there, and he asked her about it, and she had to admit it. So he had his courage built up, and he says, "So you was just down to the girl's house." So I say, "Well, if that's all she told you, she didn't tell you the good part." He says to me, "You think I won't hit you with this Thunderbird bottle?" So I knocked the Thunderbird bottle out of his hand. I didn't want to fight him, but I said to myself, "I done knocked his wine down, I better fight him now."

I: Why did you knock the bottle out of his hand?

Dox 4: To make sure he didn't hit me with the bottle. Then I hit him upside his head. And then I stomped him, and they had to get him off the sidewalk. But he didn't go to the police, because he knew he was wrong. Next time I saw him, right in this bar, he shook my hand and said, "Ain't no hard feelings."

Some respondents relied on less tangible nonverbal cues to determine whether they had been sufficiently threatened to have to resort to violence:

I: Why did you hit him?

Paul 5: He had the look. You can tell by that look. A look like, "In two seconds I am going to get busy on your ass." So I decided I better go on and blast him.

Jesse 1: My wife had to use the ladies' room . . . she brought her purse to me to watch until she comes out of the ladies' room. So I'm sitting back there, and I see this guy go in the back. No guys go in the ladies' room in Club George—we don't play that. That's about one of the most respectable places we have around here, as far as taking your lady out. Here's this guy trying to get in the door of the ladies' room. I'm hollering, telling him there's someone back there. He heard me because he looked back at me and still tried to push in on the door. So I happened to walk back there to see what his problem was. When I got back there, he was still pushing on the door. So I say, "Man, what's your problem? Didn't I tell you a lady is in there?" He said, "So what!" I said, "It's my wife." He steps back on me like he's going to square off on me. So I dropped him.

Escalating violence transcends self-defense, but it can start when one of the participants actually hits or attempts to hit the other person, who becomes entitled to self-defense:

Watson 1: When he pushed me into the wall, I turned around and I did work. I knocked him out. I had to because he was touching me.

Holt 2: He swung at me, but it missed. After it missed, I just capitalized on it. I kicked him in his nuts. Then I just went to punching him in his face. I hit him in the face numerous times. All I seen was blood gushing from his face. He stood up, and I kicked him again, and then I picked him up by his throat and dropped him. My girl, her mother, and her sister's boyfriend pulled me away from him. He got up and said, "I'm going to get you." He walked toward the car and pulled out a gun. He pointed it at me. I said, "You going to use it, you better use it." Everybody moved away, and I just stood there. Everybody said run. But I said, "I'm not running." I said, "He got that gun, and he better use it to stop me from killing him. . . ." He pointed it at me. He pulled the trigger, and it clicked and nothing happened. That's when I ran right at him, full blast. I knocked the gun down out of his hand, and I just blasted him right in the face. And he just fell out cold. Then I went home, and when I got home, I called the police.

In addition to resorting to violence to defend oneself against physical assault, some respondents believed that it matters how a man performs in a violent confrontation because his performance has reputational implications. Consequently, on some occasions violent actions were designed to minimize a man's desirability as a target of abuse in the future:

> *I:* Why don't more brothers walk away from conflict?
> *Rigsby:* If you show fear in the streets you are in trouble.

> *Troy:* They don't want the next man saying nothing to them.
> *I:* What next man?
> *Troy:* I mean, me and you fight right now. The next man, he's going to try you too. The one that lose, they are going to think he is a chump. So they want to try him too.

> *Paul:* Why are you going to walk out when tomorrow you are going to run into them again, and they are going to chop you down. If you get the reputation of being easy, then everybody thinks you are a pushover.
> *I:* Who would be an easy person?
> *Paul:* A person who says, "Man, forget it," and then walks away.

After an acquaintance insulted an ex-girlfriend of one of the respondents, the respondent asked him to apologize. The antagonist refused, and he and the respondent engaged in a brief argument that culminated in a fight when the respondent "thought he was going to pull a knife." In response to additional questioning, the respondent added that he had been motivated to use violence against the antagonist because he wanted to deter others from challenging him to fight:

> *Don Juan 2:* One of my partners came up and said, "It ain't worth it . . . just go on, man. Leave it alone." But I told him, "No, I'm tired of walking away from all of these people trying to chump me." So I hit him.
> *I:* What do you mean by "chump you"?
> *Don Juan 2:* When they pick you out as a punk . . . make you feel less than a man. Just want to come start with you . . . to see if they can beat you. It's like a challenge every time. I have to defend myself. They can't beat me.

There appears to be a shared sentiment among many men that their failure to respond with a physical assault may lead to future violations of their autonomy.

Alcohol Intoxication

Alcohol consumption was a routine feature of the respondents' activities related to hanging out in bars and bar settings. Moreover, it was not uncommon for the respondents and their peers to use alcohol, marijuana, and cocaine concurrently during the course of a particular period of hanging out.

However, very few respondents reported that they believed that pre-incident alcohol consumption or intoxication was the primary reason that they resorted to violence in a particular situation. What they did often believe, though, was that pre-incident alcohol consumption and/or intoxication could limit their capacity to tolerate or respond to rule violations committed by an antagonist:

> *Paul 1:* I take a lot of things sober, but it seems when you drink, tempers go quick. Especially when we drink heavy.

> *Hicks 1:* Well, I feel like after he had more or less verbally attacked me and pissed me off, that made me angry. And by me drinking, that made me twice as angry. Normally if I wasn't drinking, I would have just stepped off and just went on.

A few respondents reported that their pre-incident consumption of alcohol contributed to their opponent's actions, and to their opponents taking advantage of them:

> *Dox 1:* He knew I was drinking. There was no doubt about it. But he didn't have to use his knife. If I had not been drinking, I don't think he would have tried me like that. I feel like he knew he couldn't do that man to man. That's why he had to use his knife.

Respondents also considered alcohol intoxication to be responsible for others committing rule violations that they would not ordinarily have committed if they had not been under the influence:

> *Washington 1:* If he hadn't been drinking, when I said no, he probably would have accepted it and kindly turned around and walked away.

> *Mac 3:* I think the alcohol made him think he was a he-man.
> *I:* If he had not been drinking, do you think the situation would have still happened?
> *Mac 3:* No.
> *I:* What if you had not been drinking? Do you think you would have gone outside with him?
> *Mac 3:* I don't think it would have even led to that. If I had not been drinking I probably would have just left. But being that I had alcohol, the alcohol was telling me go on and do it up, because he asked for it. But this other voice was saying, "Just leave," and I tried to reason with him.

Finally, some respondents expressed the view that there was something fateful about alcohol consumption among black men hanging out in bars and bar settings leading to violent confrontations:

> *Don Juan:* When you got fifty to fifty-five people out here, they have a tendency to be drinking and doing drugs. It seems like somebody got to fight. You can come up here and just read it. People like to fight or prove something to other people out here on the streets for no reason at all. . . . It seems like when you get drunk, you want to release something from thousands of years ago. You just take it out on the first person you come across.

Violence as Communication

In many of the incidents reconstructed by the respondents, the patterns of interaction included a two-stage communication process. In stage one, the antagonist and the respondent engaged in verbal communication in which each participant attempted to make some main or primary point:

> *I:* What would you say was the main thing he was saying to you?
>
> *Patterson 1:* . . . "Your brother's going to prison, and he won't be nothing but a faggot when he gets out."
>
> *I:* And the main thing you were trying to say to him was?
>
> *Patterson 1:* "Cool out, man, before a fight or something gets started."

> *Troy 1:* I told him to stay out of my business. . . . He provoked me by talking after I told him to leave me alone.

> *Washington 1:* He was trying to say that he was thirsty like me. I guess since we knew each other, he felt like I should share my beer with him, and he wanted some beer too. The point I was trying to get across to him was that I don't have to share with him. My point was, "It's mine, I paid for it, and I don't have to share with you if I don't want to." I don't think he was listening.

> *Lonzo 1:* He just wanted me out of his lady's face. And he communicated the fact that he had no respect for me any longer, and I said that was fine.

In stage two of the communication process, there was a noticeable transition from verbal communication to violence as communication. The transition generally occurred after one of the participants had failed to provide an acceptable account of his behavior or after efforts to align disrupted relations had failed. Respondents who justified their use of violence at such junctures often saw their use of violence as a message:

> I: What were you trying to accomplish when you hit him?
> *Chast 2:* I wanted him to know that we were going to go to blows every time he acted that way toward my woman.
> I: What way was that?
> *Chast 2:* His mouth, his language, his stupidity—he was being an ass-hole. I wanted him to know that "I'm not going to let you insult me or my woman."

Another example of violence as communication is described below in the extended account of Walker:

> *Walker 1:* I wanted to embarrass him and discourage him from ever bothering me. And to show him that I would kick his ass in front of high-class people, low-class people, it don't matter to me. I wanted him to know, "If you need your ass kicked, I would give it to you.". . . I tried to end it forever by em-barrassing him. I beat him real bad. They had to reconstruct his face. I said, "You want to be an asshole," he was down on the ground begging me, "please don't hit me again." I picked him up by his hair and put his face to the junkie he was with, and I said, "Fuck you and all your junkie friends." I said, "I'm going to teach you a lesson." I said, "I don't want you to ever fuck with me again." I said, Look at your junkie friends and say, I'll never fuck with you again Mr. Walker.' " He said it twice, then I pushed his face into the cement, I opened his legs. I said, "Now I'm going to be an asshole." He had no control over his body, he was helpless, I kicked him in his fucking balls. That's how mad I was.

In the following section, factors that contribute to respondents' participation in repeated acts of violence under various circumstances are discussed.

Contingent Consistency

According to Toch, "Violent men have dispositions to react violently, and these dispositions are triggered by a limited range of situations."[4] Toch has introduced the term *contingent consistency* to refer to the repeat performance of violent conduct under various circumstances.

Many of the men I interviewed provided accounts of more than one violent confrontation in which they had been a primary participant. These accounts suggest that there were situation-specific commonalities that served as catalysts for violence participation under various circumstances. I found three contingent consistencies that were predominant in respondents' accounts of violent confrontations that occurred in bars and bar settings, including disrespect, defense of a relative or friend, and self-defense.

Disrespect

In an earlier chapter, I discussed three precipitating events that respondents tended to refer to when asked to explain the first stage in the sequence of events leading to violent confrontations in which they had been involved. The precipitating events they pointed to included loud talking and "getting bad," insults and identity attacks, and disrespect and unacceptable accounts. The perception that an antagonist had engaged in behavior demonstrating disrespect for the respondent was a salient theme for all three categories of precipitating events.

In addition to serving as a catalyst for interpersonal violence, disrespect is also a significant contingent consistency—that is, a major factor contributing to violent confrontations in which respondents felt compelled to resort to violence when their antagonist, they believed, had deliberately demonstrated disrespect for them:

> *Lee 1:* He kept bugging my woman and my sister, and they asked me to ask the brother to cut them some slack.
> *I:* How was he bugging them?
> *Lee 1:* Talking to them. Rapping to them. Trying to make plays for them, and they weren't interested. They told him that they had old men and everything. So they asked me to speak to him. So I spoke to the brother and told him that "This is my woman and this is my sister, and I would appreciate it if you didn't bother them." And then he disrespected me. He said, "What the fuck you got to do with it? What do you want to do?" So I told the brother, "Let's go outside." So he came outside and the fight was on.
> *I:* Why did you go outside?
> *Lee 1:* Because he got loud and totally disrespected me. That's why I asked him to go outside. I was mad, and I was ready to fight.

Disrespect was also a salient theme in another incident in which this respondent provided an account. The confrontation occurred after a friend of the respondent attempted to mediate an argument between the respondent and his girlfriend. On two occasions prior to the violent confrontation between the respondent and the antagonist, the respondent had told his friend not to intervene when he and his girlfriend were arguing:

Lee 3: Three weeks went past before he and I got into it. Me and my girlfriend would be arguing, and he would always come over and get me, intervening with me and my woman's argument. And I had asked him prior to that, twice before, "Brother when me and my woman are arguing, stay out of my business, man. The next time you come over, you and I are going to have to fight."

In his account of the incident in which he and his friend fought, the respondent attributed his aggressive actions to anger precipitated by the antagonist's failure to respect his wishes concerning the management of his relationships with his girlfriend:

Lee 3: I initiated the contact because I threw a drink in his face.
   I: Why did you do that?
Lee 3: Because as a man, what I say to him, tell him, or explain has no importance, whatsoever. He totally disrespected me. I asked him not to do it, and I even let him know that if he did continue doing it, that we were going to fight. I just felt like he was totally disrespecting me as a friend, as a partner, and as a brother. And most of all, making me feel like I couldn't handle my own problem or my own life. It was my woman, not his, and it made me mad.

Defense of a Relative or Friend

Another major factor contributing to violent confrontations between black men in bars and bar settings was an antagonist's refusal to provide an acceptable account of actions he had directed against a relative or friend of a respondent. Regarding contingent consistencies, some respondents were very aware of their disposition and vulnerability to becoming involved in violent confrontations in which they felt duty-bound to defend a relative or friend:

Paul: I don't disrespect women. That's probably my biggest problem. That's why I get into so many fights. Most of the time I get into a fight, it has been about a woman. I am always sticking up for them or defending them. Other than that, I don't have any trouble.

The most conventional dispositions contributing to recurrent involvement in violent confrontations are norms in which duties and roles are heavily prescribed. For example, one respondent provided accounts of three incidents in which one of his brothers was involved in either a heated argument or violent confrontation and the respondent attempted to intervene. In one incident he was stabbed, in another he was hit in the face with a board and subsequently knocked out. In his accounts of these incidents, the respondent expressed the view that he felt compelled to assist his brothers when they were in trouble. He also noted that one of his brothers was very aware of the respondent's sense of brotherly loyalty and used it to his advantage in calculating his behavior when he wanted to transform a heated argument into a violent confrontation:

> *Germ 1:* My brother got into an incident with his ex-girlfriend. I went to stop him. He slapped the girl. But I knew if I didn't turn around and talk to my brother, he wouldn't hit her and go off on [have a violent confrontation with] her brother. My brother is like this. He goes off when he knows that I am around and that he got my attention. He will go off quicker. A lot of times people will say, "Your brother is over there arguing." So I turn my back. Nine times out of ten, he won't fight. But when I turn around to see what's happening, he goes off.

In situations in which respondents repeatedly resorted to violence to defend a relative or friend, the decision to fight was often influenced by an overt sense of personal loyalty and responsibility:

> *Butch:* Right or wrong, I am always in their [relatives'] corner. I always feel one way, and that is, they are right.
> *I:* Are they always right?
> *Butch:* In my eyes and in my heart, they are always right.

Some of the respondents defined manhood in terms of their willingness to resort to violence to defend a relative or friend:

> *Butch 1:* I am one hundred percent man, and if anybody ever disrespects anybody that I love, I got to go and see about it. I am a champ, and I love my family.

This respondent provided accounts of two incidents in which he had intervened to defend a relative. In one of the incidents, the former girlfriend of his nephew, whom he referred to as his niece, came to his home and informed him that a man that she was no longer dating had come to her residence when she wasn't home and threatened and cursed at her children:

> *Butch 1:* He came there, and evidently he knew that the mother wasn't home. He's going to come there and beat on the window and this and that. The children were telling him that "my mother's not home." That's when he starting calling them bitches and this and that. He said, "If you don't let me in the house, I will take my hammer." He has a habit of toting a hammer around, right. And he said, if they didn't open up the door, he was going

to break the door down. He was going to beat them all over the head with a hammer.

Even though the police had been called and the respondent's niece had secured a restraining order that prohibited the antagonist from coming near her residence, the respondent felt compelled to approach the antagonist when he saw him on the street:

Butch 1: I love my nieces. They don't have a father that lives with them. So I took it upon myself to go over and ask the guy why did he do what he did to my nieces. And when I asked him about why he approached my niece and the little kids, he said, "Man, motherfuck the little bitches."

I: How did you feel when he said that?

Butch 1: I felt like a shitty poppa. Because I didn't feel like they were bitches. So my mind just went ill. My mind just went on the run. So I took my knife and I just cut him about twenty-five to thirty times.

In another incident, this respondent reported that he felt compelled to resort to violence in defense of his girlfriend who was being beaten on a street corner by a man with whom she had been arguing:

Butch 2: I happened to be upstairs doing a crossword puzzle book. Then my son came up there, and he said, "The guy's got Mommy on the ground," and this guy was trying to stab my woman in the face with a knife. So I get up an' close the crossword puzzle book and go out into the street. When I get down there I take my coat and glasses off. . . . So they tell me he's got a gun. I say, "Homeboy, you better shoot me before I get to you." I said, "You had my woman on the ground." He said, "Man, motherfuck you and that bitch." But he got too close to me, and the next thing I knew I had a knife around his neck and I cut his throat. So he runs out in traffic and says, "Yeah, man, you got me." I said, "Hey, man, you can come here, I ain't through cutting you." He had my woman down on the ground trying to stab her in the face and beating her head on the ground for no reason at all, and [he] don't even know her.

Accounts of incidents motivated by a desire to defend a relative or friend suggest that two catalysts or precipitating factors converge and lead some violent black men to become involved in repeated acts of violence in these situations. The specific catalysts include, first, the internalization of a deeply entrenched sense of duty and responsibility that allows for the use of violence against individuals who insult or assault one's relatives or friends, and, second, the perception that an antagonist has deliberately demonstrated a lack of respect for the individual who intervenes in a situation to defend a relative or friend.

Self-Defense

Repeated involvement in situations in which respondents resorted to violence because they believed that an antagonist threatened their physical safety is the third and final contingency consistency observed in the respondents' accounts. Violence participation as self-defense was justified as being an appropriate way to avoid physical injury, as well as morally right.

> *Watson 1:* I knocked him out. I had to because he was touching me, I don't touch nobody, nobody touches me. When somebody touch me, trying to physically hurt me, it's like I fear for my life when I'm fighting with somebody.
>
> *I:* Was there any rule that he violated that caused this whole situation to go off?
>
> *Watson 1:* Yeah: "Don't touch me."
>
> *I:* Why is that significant?
>
> *Watson 1:* Because I don't know what he could do to me, or how he would have tried to hurt me. I don't want to get hurt, don't touch me. If you don't touch me, it's okay. . . . I figure if they force themselves to have problems with me, I have to protect me, whatever way it comes.

This respondent was considered to be one of the most prolific fighters in the community. He attributed his overt predisposition to resort to violence to what he had learned from an incident in which his cousin was killed in a greasy spoon restaurant:

> *Watson 1:* They are trying to hurt everybody out here, like my cousin, Alco. He died in my arms that day at Miss Ethel's. He wasn't fighting anyone. When they touched him, he turned around and died. So now when I fight, I fight to protect me now.
>
> *I:* Because you're concerned that . . .
>
> *Watson 1:* That it could happen to me.

In some situations, resorting to violence as self-defense is gratuitous. For example, in the incident Watson 2, the respondent was having an argument with his girlfriend in one of the bars when a close friend of his girlfriend aggressively intervened. While the respondent's initial motive for resorting to violence appears to have been self-defense, his gratuitous use of violence reflects a deeply entrenched acceptance of violence as a means of resolving interpersonal conflict:

> *Watson 2:* Me and her was arguing a little bit. . . . So I was getting up to walk out the door, and her supposed-to-be cousin, he's really a friend, grabbed me by my arm, and when I turned around, he punched me in my face. . . . I was shocked—I was dazed—I didn't know what was going on. I was catching myself so I wouldn't fall out. So when I hit him, I couldn't really function just to hit him. So I picked up the cigarette machine and slammed in on his face.
>
> *I:* What do you mean, you "couldn't function to hit him"?
>
> *Watson 2:* I didn't have enough function just to go square off and hit him because I couldn't see. So I grabbed the biggest thing that was there to pick up and slammed it on him.
>
> *I:* Because you couldn't focus?
>
> *Watson 2:* Right.

Closure: The Termination of Interpersonal Conflict

Violent confrontations evolve and terminate within various interpretive and contextual boundaries. I will use the term *closure* to refer to the termination or ending of a conflict between individuals who have engaged in a potentially violent argument or an actual violent confrontation. Closure is primarily a product of evaluative definitions of specific types of social interactions that occur between violent participants, subsequent to their involvement in a confrontation.

The respondents that I interviewed provided accounts of three types of closure: symbolic, overt, and internal.

Symbolic Closure

Symbolic closure involved the recognition that a violent confrontation was over, based on an assessment of nonverbal cues and/or routine activity changes. The predominant nonverbal indicator of symbolic closure involved a situation in which, subsequent to a violent confrontation, the participants refrained from initiating any type of verbal or physical contact with each other:

> *Germ 2:* I knew I wasn't going out there to start no trouble. So long as they didn't say anything to me, it wasn't going to be no trouble. And I knew they weren't going to say nothing to me, not unless I ran into them.

I: How did you know they weren't going to say anything?
Germ 2: Because I know they wasn't.

Mac 3: I saw him in the bar.
I: Did he say anything to you?
Mac 3: No.
I: Did you say anything to him?
Mac 3: No. That was just like it was squashed, really.
I: No dialogue communicated that it was over?
Mac 3: Right. There hasn't been any words or anything since then.

Overt Closure

Arguments and violent confrontations were also brought to a conclusion by means of overt closure. By overt closure, I mean an interpersonal process in which individuals who had previously engaged in a potentially violent argument or an actual violent confrontation attempted to align or restore disrupted relations by making light of their conflict or apologizing to one another. Respondents saw overt closure as a more valid indication than symbolic closure that a particular incident was over:

I: What happened when you saw him again?
Lee 3: I saw him again about three days later. We didn't approach each other. We just looked at each other. . . . We stopped speaking for six or seven months.
I: Were you concerned that you and he were going to get into it again?
Lee 3: No, I felt bad that our friendship was shattered a little bit. I knew that I wasn't going to confront him with violence, and I knew that he knew better, by me and him being partners and friends, that it wouldn't be a good idea for him to come to confront me with anything.
I: When did you and he talk again?
Lee 3: Six or seven months after that.
I: Who approached whom?
Lee 3: We really approached each other. We started talking about things in general. And after about a couple of months, we talked about that night and the incident. He had to do thirty days in jail for hitting my sister. And I was teasing him about that. And then he asked me, "You were really going to stick me with that knife?" I said, "Yeah, I was going to stick you." Everything was squashed, and we laughed about it.
I: When was it really over?

Lee 3: When we both admitted our wrongness.

I: What did you and he admit was wrong?

Lee 3: I admitted I was wrong for throwing a drink in his face and even telling a friend something like what I said. And he admitted that he was wrong for . . . even though I'm his best friend and we hang out every day, you have to give a man some space from time to time. He apologized for not giving me that space.

When overt closure occurred by one violent participant apologizing to the other, the conversation usually took place on the first or second encounter in a bar or bar setting:

Washington 1: The next time I ran into him was, I think, outside the same bar. He walked up and said, "Hey, man, I'm sorry about the other night." He said, he really didn't mean it, he said, "I was drunk.". . . We talked a little bit. He said there was no excuse for it, and he was sorry. I told him that's okay. . . .

I: How did you feel about him apologizing?

Washington 1: It made me feel a little better. I think he realized that he had done something wrong.

Internal Closure

A few men expressed the view that the incident was over immediately after they had physically dominated their antagonist. For these men, closure was largely an intrapersonal process in which they interpreted their own victory over an antagonist as constituting closure. This situation is one of internal closure, because the sense of closure occurs internally, within one participant, and does not rely on a symbolic or overt exchange involving antagonists. A respondent usually experienced closure at the time of his verbal or physical domination of the antagonist:

I: At what point did you realize that this situation was really over?

Watson 1: I knew the situation was over when I knocked him out.

I: Why did you know it was over then?

Watson 1: Because he don't have enough heart to come back to do it again while he was sober.

I: What about when he went and got his relatives?

Watson 1: I still knew it was over then. If the relatives were going to do something, they would have come on in and got me. I had put fear in their heart before they got to me.

Troy: Once I fight somebody and we both let go and I go my way, it's over with. Until it comes down to that point that he puts his hands on me again.

As a subsample of the total group of respondents, men who reported they had experienced internal closure tended to be in their early to mid-twenties at the time I interviewed them. Other respondents and others in the neighborhood regarded these men as being among the most prolific and successful fighters.

However, while the men experiencing internal closure regarded their domination and victory over their antagonist as conclusive, they were aware that closure could be ratified by symbolic and overt gestures or behaviors:

I: When you saw him again, what happened?
Troy 3: The next day he came to me. He apologized.
I: What did he say?
Troy 3: He said, "Troy, I was wrong, and it will never happen again."

Respondents attributed meanings to their antagonists' character based on the manner in which they sought to establish closure. For example, to apologize for being "wrong" was considered to be a sign of "being a man":

Troy 3: I felt as though he was a man to come forward and say he was wrong.

Moreover, in situations in which an antagonist apologized, respondents reported that they felt compelled to accept the apology:

Watson 2: He came to me like a man. He apologized and everything. I accepted his apology because the way he was acting was wrong.

Closure Resistance

Attempts to bring about closure sometimes met with personal resistance from the participants. In the incident described below, the respondent intervened in a situation to break up an argument between a friend of his and another man. After other third parties intervened and held the respondent's friend in order to prevent a physical confrontation, the respondent asked the antagonist to go outside with him to talk about the situation. As soon as the respondent and the antagonist stepped outside, the antagonist hit the respondent in the mouth with a pair of brass knuckles. The respondent was knocked out and badly injured, requiring medical care. Subsequently, the antagonist left the scene, and the respondent did not see him again until a month later. When the respondent saw the antagonist again, he approached him and initiated a conversation in which he asked for an account. According to the respondent, the primary reason he had approached the antagonist was to effect alignment and closure:

> *Jesse 2:* So I said, "What was the purpose of you hitting me in my mouth?" And he told me I should have been minding my own business. I said, "I'm gonna make it my business." That's when he stepped back on me and lifted his jacket, for I could see his piece.
>
> *I:* Did he pull the piece?
>
> *Jesse 2:* He just put his hand on it. He let me see it. He let me know he had it.
>
> *I:* So what was he trying to say to you at that point?
>
> *Jesse 2:* "You make one wrong move, and your ass is gonna be burnt." That's what he was saying in so many ways.
>
> *I:* What did you do then?
>
> *Jesse 2:* I ain't no fool. I backed up and continued doing what I was doing.
>
> *I:* Is that how it ended?
>
> *Jesse 2:* I wouldn't really say it ended. The first wrong move he makes—he don't have too much of nothing to say or do to me—and it will be on.
>
> *I:* How would you describe the relationship you had with him?
>
> *Jesse 2:* I really don't have no relationship with him, because I don't want nothing to do with him. Nothing at all, because I know what it's gonna be when he get out of place with me.
>
> *I:* What is it going to be?
>
> *Jesse 2:* An all-out war.

Post-Incident Effects

Failure to establish closure had post-incident effects that influenced the later construction of routine orientations and routine activities related to hanging out in bars and bar settings.

I asked each of the respondents to comment on how his involvement in a violent confrontation had subsequently affected his routine activities. Post-incident effects are changes in routine activities that occur after a violent confrontation.

The most significant factor influencing post-incident routine activities was the respondent's determination of whether closure had occurred. Respondents tended to refer to their psychological orientation as well as offer descriptions of the concrete changes, or lack of them, in routine activities associated with hanging out in bars and bar settings. Four categories of post-incident effects were observed in respondents' accounts, including anticipation of violence, transsituational conflict, packing a weapon, and changes in routine activities.

Anticipation of Violence

A salient theme in the accounts in which closure had not been established was the anticipation of violence between the respondent and his antagonist at some other time or place:

> *I:* When you started going down to Dot's again, were you concerned that something might jump off?
>
> *Washington 1:* I felt like he might have some kind of animosity toward me, since they had escorted him out of the bar. I didn't know what was going on in his mind. That's why I was a little worried. . . . I said to myself, "Proceed with caution." I was thinking that I wanted to be prepared this time.

The anticipation of violence was reinforced for some respondents, when others would tell them or they would observe for themselves that their antagonist was visibly carrying weapons:

> *Dox 2:* I just seen him, and he has a hammer in his pocket. He's in the same place [a bar about fifty yards away from the bar in which the interview was conducted and where the respondent and antagonist had fought a week before], and I feel like that's for me.

Anticipation of violent retaliation could be overwhelming, particularly for those men who had been involved in multiple incidents within a short span of time:

> *Dox 3:* I got to go to court for knocking one boy out. I got to go to court for getting knocked in the head and cut. Man, I'm looking for somebody to take me away from here. Just for a month, anything. Because this is nothing.

This respondent had been involved in three separate incidents in the week before I interviewed him. On the day prior to the interview, he had been cut across the neck. On the day I interviewed him, a former antagonist was carrying a hammer on the street. And on the day after the interview, another one of his antagonists reported to me that he was hanging on the street with a baseball bat in anticipation of further conflict with the respondent:

> *I:* After the incident had happened and you were arrested and you got out of jail, were you at all concerned that you might have to have another confrontation with him?
>
> *Rigsby 1:* Yeah, because he had said some things to my sister.
>
> *I:* What did he say?
>
> *Rigsby 1:* He called her names . . . she told me.
>
> *I:* Was he trying to send you a message?
>
> *Rigsby 1:* Yeah, what he was going to do to me in the future.
>
> *I:* Did you do anything extra to protect yourself after you got out of jail?
>
> *Rigsby 1:* No more than I always did. First, I came home. Then I got my bat. Then I went to Jack's Swap Shop to buy another knife. [The police had confiscated the knife he used to cut Dox with.] Then I took the bat home.
>
> *I:* Why did you take the bat up on State Street?
>
> *Rigsby 1:* Because I had no other weapon.
>
> *I:* Were you concerned that you might run into Dox on State Street and he would have a weapon?
>
> *Rigsby 1:* I did run into him out there, and I had the bat.
>
> *I:* Did he say anything to you?
>
> *Rigsby 1:* No.
>
> *I:* Did you say anything to him?
>
> *Rigsby 1:* We just stared each other down—that's it.
>
> *I:* Did you have the bat for him?
>
> *Rigsby 1:* If I needed it.

Respondents generally believed that it was common sense to be alert to the possibility that an antagonist might attempt to retaliate at some point after the initial incident. Thus, the anticipation of violence represented a shared expectation regarding the potential consequences associated with violence participation:

> *Jesse:* Anytime you have a run-in with a person, you have to watch that person. You never know what's on his mind. You don't know if he's going to come back to get revenge. You just don't know. This is something that you have to be aware of.
>
> *I:* Do you think other brothers think the same thing?
>
> *Jesse:* If they don't, they're stupid. That's how you get a lot of brothers stabbed, cut up, beaten half to death—by not thinking, by not watching their backs, by not being alert. You know you had this

run-in with this guy, you know how it came out, now you got to be on the aggressive side.

Anticipation of violence could be mitigated by overt or symbolic acts of closure. Symbolic acts signaling closure caused this respondent not to anticipate additional violence between his antagonist and himself:

> *I:* Were you concerned that a physical confrontation was going to occur between you and him or you and his brother after the incident happened?
>
> *Paul 1:* No. Just for that day. If they were going to do something, they were going to do it that day. . . . I passed by them a couple of times, and I watched my back. He never said anything to me, and I never said anything to him. . . . I knew it was all over with then. He had nothing to say. He kept going and I kept going.

Transsituational Conflict

Joint consideration of findings related to closure and post-incident effects suggest that when respondents and their antagonists failed to establish closure, this would sometimes lead to transsituational conflict: that is, a dispute that initially occurred in a particular situational context that was subsequently carried over into other situational contexts:

> *Joey 1:* We fought for a whole week. Every time we saw each other we fought.

> *Paul 1:* We fought for a month after that. They chased me home a couple of times with a shotgun.

A typical transsituational conflict in the respondents' accounts included at least two encounters in which respondent and antagonist would either argue or argue and fight. Respondent Ozell, for example, provided an account of transsituational conflict that occurred between himself and several antagonists who were related. During a three-month period the respondent and his antagonists were involved in several loud arguments and two incidents in which physical violence occurred. Overt closure did not occur until a year and a half after the first incident.

The precipitating event involved an incident in which the respondent's 40-year-old sister was jumped and knocked unconscious by a group of three or four men and one woman. During the assault, one of the perpetrators jammed a stick into the victim's vagina. After two days of hospitalization, the respondent's sister regained consciousness and informed him as well as the police that she had been hit over the head and beaten by three or four males and one female. She identified the males as members of a family well known in the community. Three weeks after the incident, the police had not arrested any of the persons identified by his sister. Subsequently, the respondent became increasingly frustrated and decided to seek justice through his own initiative.

The first incident occurred after the respondent approached one of the men whom his sister identified as one of the perpetrators who jumped her. According to the respondent, he wanted to talk to the people his sister had identified in order to determine whether they had committed the act and why:

> *Ozell 1:* I knew I was going to have to approach them, and I wanted to approach them in a humble manner. I was walking near Dee Dee's Lounge. The person I wanted to approach was Doug, because my sister had mentioned his name more so than any other person who was at the scene. Plus, he was the oldest of the brothers. . . . So I approached him. I figured he might be more mature about the situation than his younger brother. I waved at him, as usual. So he said, "Somebody said that you wanted to talk to me." He said, "I'm going to park and come over to Dee Dee's." I went on over there. I'm preprogrammed.
>
> *I:* Preprogrammed to do what?
> *Ozell 1:* To deal with it straight up.
> *I:* To talk about it?
> *Ozell 1:* That's the first thing. If talking can't get anywhere . . . to get the situation solved, one way or another.
> *I:* How did you get on the subject?
> *Ozell 1:* That was the number-one thing out of his mouth. He said, "I'm sorry about what happened to your sister, but I had nothing to do with it." I say, "Well, she did say that you and your brothers did have something to do with it." He said, "I'm not my brother," and I look at him eye to eye and I said, "In the name of Jesus Christ, I hope you didn't have anything to do with it." We go back too far, we go back to Cub Scouts. I went on to relate to him how close-knit his family and our family is. He said, "I wouldn't do anything like that." So I walks away. I said, "Okay, thank you, but I will find out who did it."

On leaving the bar, the respondent reported that several of the antagonist's relatives and friends were present, both in the bar and outside in front of the bar:

> *Ozell 1:* As I stepped out the door, I noticed that he had about seven or eight people there. I turned to go, and I saw his mother coming

across the street. She had a four-foot iron pipe in her hand. She was trying to hit me over the back of my head with it. So as she went to hit me, I twirled around, I grabbed the pipe, took the pipe. So then I left myself exposed to Doug. He stabbed me in the back. When I took the pipe from her, it fell on the ground. When it fell to the ground, another one of her sons came up. When he came up, me and him went for the pipe. So he picked up the pipe and was swinging it at me.

The first incident in this transsituational conflict ended when the police arrived and broke it up. The respondent was taken to the hospital and treated for knife wounds.

Immediately after the incident was broken up, the antagonists went to the police station and filed an assault complaint against the respondent. At his second court appearance, the judge found the respondent not guilty.

Three weeks after the first incident, the respondent and his antagonists were involved in another confrontation. The second incident occurred in Frank's, one of the after-hours joints. According to the respondent, he had seen the primary antagonist of the second incident—Herman, another one of the brothers whom the sister had identified—earlier that evening in Dee Dee's Lounge. At that time, he felt that the antagonist, Herman, was aggravated by his presence:

Ozell 2: He and I are in Dee Dee's Lounge. So Herman sees me, and his facial expression changes. Before he saw me, he was partying and all happy. Then all of a sudden, he's nervous, keyed up, can't sit still as long as I'm watching him. I wasn't watching him directly, but he knew that I knew he was in the bar. So the bar closes at two A.M., and a lot of people go across the street to Frank's place. In Frank's, he walks past me and says, "What you keep looking at me for?". . . I didn't say anything to him. I ignored him. He goes back over to his friends. They are making statements. He points at me and says, "I'm going to get you." So then one of his brothers came and started trying to calm him down.

I: Was he getting loud?

Ozell 2: Yeah, like a wild dog on a chain.

I: So then what happens?

Ozell 2: He got a little worse, and a couple hours later their mother came in.

I: What do you mean, "he got a little worse"?

Ozell 2: He got more antagonistic. He was raging and just fired up. He wanted to tear into me.

I: So how did that situation end?

Ozell 2: Frank told me to stay in the back room until I cooled out. I had gotten so angry, tears had come out of one eye—that's when I get supermad.

    I: Did Frank ever tell them to leave or anything?

Ozell 2: The reason why he didn't is because his brother and his mother were taking him out of the place.

    I: Why did Frank tell you to go in the back then?

Ozell 2: To separate the two of us. If this guy breaks loose from his relatives and attacks me, he got to run way back there. But if I'm in there where he is, he might be more apt to break loose and make one little hit at me. He didn't want anything to go down.

According to the respondent, the second incident did not result in violence primarily because the antagonist, Herman, allowed himself to be restrained and persuaded not to fight the respondent. Also, the respondent did not feel compelled to respond to the antagonist's threats by resorting to violence.

A third incident occurred between the respondent and the primary antagonist of the second incident, Herman, shortly after he left the after-hours joint at daybreak:

Ozell 3: I waited there till daybreak. It must have been eight in the morning when I left Frank's place. There was a woman out on the street that I use to fool around with. She and I were talking when I saw Herman walking on the opposite side of the street. When I saw him, I started to cross the street and go over there to meet him. All of a sudden I heard a noise. He threw a gasoline firebomb at me. Then he reached into a brown bag and pulled out another one, put fire to it, and threw it at me. Then he threw a third one at me. When he threw the last one, he closed his bag and got ready to take off. He went into these tall bushes behind the body shop. The grass was tall, and I wasn't going to run in there after him. I turned around and came back, and somebody had called the fire department.

    I: Was a building on fire?

Ozell 3: Yeah. So I identified him—he was already on probation. They sent him back to prison.

Termination of conflict between this respondent and his antagonists began to occur after the primary antagonist of the second and third incidents was arrested and incarcerated for throwing firebombs at the respondent. Three weeks after the antagonist was incarcerated, the respondent was arrested and incarcerated for committing an assault against an antagonist who had not been involved in the incidents of the transsituational conflict. According to the respondent, shortly after he was incarcerated in the county jail, the antagonist, Herman, sent the respondent a letter in which he claimed that only one of his brothers had been involved in the incident in which the respondent's sister was beaten. He also stated that the brother who was involved was not Doug, the primary antagonist of the first incident (Ozell 1).

A year and a half after the first incident, the feud and the anticipation of violence ended with the antagonists initiating overt closure:

> I: How did the situation finally end?
>
> Ozell 3: One by one, they came to me and apologized. Even Germ, the one who swung the pipe at me, apologized. He said, "Man, I know you didn't body-slam my mother."
>
> I: What about their mom? Did she ever apologize to you?
>
> Ozell 3: Indirectly, she started saying good things about me and trying to make me look good in the eyes of others instead of trying to abuse me as if I'm some kind of street criminal or some gangster.

This typical account of a transsituational conflict suggest that closure is a major stage in the interpersonal process associated not only with single incidents but with transsituational confrontations among black men.

In addition to the anticipation of violence that was associated with participants' failure to establish closure, transsituational conflict was also influenced by anger and a desire to retaliate for something that occurred during the original incident:

> Paul 2: I thought we had an understanding about everything, but Junior was still upset because I had cut him in the face with a wine bottle. So he was determined to get me.

Packing a Weapon

Some men responded to their involvement in a violent confrontation in which closure had not occurred by arming themselves. Carrying a weapon following their participation in a violent confrontation is a concrete manifestation of their perception that closure has not been established and they should therefore anticipate violence in the future:

> I: Were you concerned that you were going to have to deal with these people in the future?
>
> Hawkins 1: Yes.
>
> I: Did you do anything extra to protect yourself?

Hawkins 1: I got my pistol.
        I: Were you carrying it?
Hawkins 1: At all times.

In incidents in which an antagonist had either displayed or used a weapon against a respondent, respondents expressed a sense of immediacy about securing a weapon to protect themselves:

Johnny B. 1: On the day I got out of the hospital, I went around to my cousin's house, and he put a gun in my hand, and I came up on the street.
        I: Why did you take the gun?
Johnny B. 1: They were trying to kill me. I needed it for defensive purposes.
        I: How long did you carry the gun after the incident happened?
Johnny B. 1: About a good two to three months. When I would come up here, I would walk across the street and stash it in the parking lot next door to the bar.

Subsequent to a confrontation in which closure had not occurred, some men entered the bar settings and stashed weapons in bushes, trash cans, or parking lots in order to be prepared to confront enemies they might encounter while hanging out.

        I: After the first incident, were you concerned about encountering these people in the future?
Ozell 1: Yes.
        I: Did you start carrying a weapon?
Ozell 1: No, but I planted one.
        I: Where?
Ozell 1: Outside the bar.
        I: Why did you do that?
Ozell 1: I knew they were carrying them because I had an encounter with Andy, and he put one in my face.

The purpose of stashing the weapon was to have it immediately available. The respondent quoted below let it be known to the bar owner with whom he had had an initial dispute that he was packing a gun. Stashing the gun was a compromise resolution. The gun was a deterrent, and the stashing would reduce the risk of being arrested if someone were to inform the police that he was carrying a gun. Respondents also saw stashing a weapon as a way to reduce criminal liability if they were to use it:

       I: Why would you stash it rather than keep it on you?

Johnny B. 1: Number one, people call the police on you, and the gun was registered, and it was my cousin's. But if I run over there and somebody happens to be chasing me and I run over there to it, I can say I found it. I just picked it up and shot it. But if they say I pulled it out of my pocket, then they would say I planned it.

A respondent who had been stabbed in the chest provided the following rationale to explain why he never left home without his knife or some other weapon:

Hicks 1: It's a crowded situation up on State Street. You've got four bars, they got noplace else to go but there. There's plenty of alcohol, there's plenty of drugs, there's plenty of reefer. When you mix all that together, somebody's going off. And I don't want to be the victim, which I happened to become that time.

    I: When you started hanging out in the street after you were stabbed, did you start carrying your weapon again?

Hicks 1: Oh, yes. Never leave home without it.

    I: Why is that?

Hicks 1: I know how it is out in the streets. It's dog eat dog. Any moment, it could happen. You could get stabbed, shot, cut, and it's best to have something with you. There ain't no more of them fair fights.

    I: Why aren't there any fair fights?

Hicks 1: They don't have time to sit there and go forty rounds with you, when they can stick your guts or hit you across your throat and make a long story short. Now lately, they're carrying pistols and what not. What are you going to do—hold your hand up and talk about a fair fight?

Changes in Routine Activities

Participation in a violent confrontation was a major event in the lives of these respondents and on their routine activities.

Many respondents reported that they did not substantially change their patterns of hanging out in bars and bar settings following their participation in a violent confrontation. The most common reason they gave for why they had not changed their hanging-out patterns was incident closure. That is, the perception that some type of closure had been established precluded the anticipation of violence between their antagonists and themselves in the future. In an account of an incident that occurred in Frank's (the after-hours joint), for example, a respondent described an incident in which early closure had led him not to anticipate violence in the future or to change his routine activities.

An argument between the respondent and one of his drinking buddies occurred after the drinking buddy directed an overt sexual invitation toward one of the respondent's ex-girlfriends. The respondent objected to the comment and asked the antagonist to apologize. The argument escalated into a physical confrontation in which the respondent claimed he knocked the antagonist out after the antagonist put his hands in his pocket during the verbal exchange. The respondent reported that he did not consider changing his routine activities, because closure was established shortly after the confrontation occurred:

> *I:* So when he woke up, what happened? Did anybody go to his aid or try to wake him up?
>
> *Don Juan 1:* A couple of people went and helped him up, walked him around, and he went down the street. He went to Miss Ethel's [a twenty-four-hour greasy spoon restaurant and gambling parlor] and stayed down there. They told him what happened, and he came back down the street with a stick. So I thought he was going to fight again, but he just walked up to me and said, "Yo, what happened?" I said, "You was drunk, man, and you tried me. I just defended myself, I hit you, I knocked you out."

This incident was terminated as a result of a verbal exchange in which respondent and antagonist negotiated closure:

> *Don Juan 1:* He said, "But you snuck me." I told him, "When you talk to me eye-to-eye and stick your hands in your pocket, you told me you was gonna fuck me up, you wanna fight . . . so I did the first thing that came to my mind—knock you out before you could pull out your pocket what you got."
>
> *I:* So how did all that talk end?
>
> *Don Juan 1:* He got respect for me, I got respect for him as a man.
>
> *I:* How did you get respect from him? When you told him that you didn't sneak him, what happened then?
>
> *Don Juan 1:* He said, "Well, I really couldn't tell you if you snuck me or not, but that's what somebody else said." He said, "I know you from the past. We just got through getting drunk together." He said, "I will just call it even—we'll squash it." We squashed it after that.
>
> *I:* So did you feel it was over at that point?
>
> *Don Juan 1:* Yes.
>
> *I:* And did he go his separate way that night, or did you all

have some more drinks after that, or did you go about your business or what?

Don Juan 1: I went on about my business, and he went about his business.

I: Were you at all concerned that you might have another encounter with him in the future, or did you think that it was over because he had apologized?

Don Juan 1: I thought it was over.

Another major reason that respondents gave for not changing their hanging-out patterns after participating in a violent confrontation was that they were not afraid of their antagonist:

I: Did you stop coming up to Ann's World or the other bar that you frequent?

Paul 1: Do you mean did I avoid him? No, I didn't.

I: Why not?

Paul 1: I'm not afraid of him or his family.

Some respondents reported that they did not change their hanging-out patterns because they wanted their antagonists to know that they were willing to fight again if the antagonist chose to initiate additional conflict:

Kessler 1: I went home and checked my firearms. My concern was that if he started something, I wanted to be ready because he had pulled a knife on me the first time. So I had made plans.

I: Are you saying that if you saw him again in the future, you were planning on fighting him again?

Kessler 1: Right. Whatever the circumstances.

A second encounter between this respondent and antagonist never took place, partly because two and a half weeks later the antagonist was arrested for stabbing a man to death in a greasy spoon restaurant.

Among respondents who did change their hanging-out patterns after participating in a fight in a bar or bar setting, the most common reason for doing so that they gave was to avoid additional violence between themselves and their antagonists. The decision was primarily influenced by respondents' perception that closure had not been established, and therefore they anticipated that they and their antagonists were likely to engage in additional acts of violence in the future:

Germ 1: I haven't been there since this happened. . . . I figured if I came back the next night and they were there, it would be the same thing all over again.

Continuing either to hang out in or to deliberately avoid bars and bar settings after participating in a violent confrontation had symbolic significance. To continue to hang out, for example, might signal that a man was not afraid of his antagonist and was willing to engage in additional acts of violence. Avoiding bars and bar settings, by contrast, might be done to signal an individual's lack of interest in participating in additional acts of violence:

Washington 1: Lots of times I'll quit going to a bar or an area where I have got into a fight. I call it keeping myself out of trouble. Because if you go in there a couple of hours later or the next day, people have a tendency to believe that you are looking for trouble. I learned this from experience.

Respondents also attributed meanings to noticeable changes in an antagonist's routine patterns of hanging out. For example, an antagonist who appeared to be avoiding the bars, street corners, poolrooms, gambling parlors, and other public settings where he generally hung out might be perceived as attempting to communicate symbolic closure:

Watson 1: When I didn't see him around, it made me more alert to the fact that it was over.

Respondents also associated overt changes in routine activities with an escalation of the seriousness of the confrontation. For example, in incidents in which a respondent inflicted or suffered a severe injury, hanging-out patterns were interrupted by hospitalization or incarceration:

I: After this happened, did you continue to hang out up at Frank's and up on State Street with the same degree of regularity as you did before?

Hicks 1: I had to shut down for a while because I was in the process of trying to heal. . . . I was in the hospital for about three weeks.

I: How serious were the injuries?

Hicks 1: Real bad. I stayed in critical condition for about nine days. Then after that, I came here and stayed with my mother for a while, just to get away from everything, you know, for about two months. Finally, I came out. I stopped drinking and doing everything.

I: Why were you doing that?

Hicks 1: Because you have to slow down and get your bearings. I'm trying to heal, and my body's all messed up—puttin' alcohol in it wouldn't help.

I: So that's why you were lying low?

Hicks 1: Yeah.

    I: So you were lying low to heal or to stay out of trouble?

Hicks 1: I was lying low to heal. He was in jail, so I wasn't worried about him.

    I: After the stabbing occurred, what was the most significant change in your lifestyle?

Turner 1: Going to prison.

    I: How much time did you do for this?

Turner 1: Six and a half years all together, out of ten. I did three and a half years before being released on parole. I got paroled twice and got violated twice.

The respondents tended to make a distinction between changes in routine activities and changes in routine orientations. That is, in response to questions designed to uncover how they categorized and interpreted post-incident effects related to violence participation, most respondents made a distinction between routine activities as behavior and routine activities as a psychological state or consciousness. For example, most of the respondents reported that they continued to frequent bars and bar settings following their involvement in a violent confrontation. While most did not substantially change the frequency of their hanging-out patterns, many of them did modify their style of hanging out. One way in which they did this was by stashing or packing weapons when they frequented bars and bar settings.

Regarding routine orientations toward hanging out in bars and bar settings, as we saw in Chapter 5, respondents tended to define lower-class black bars and bar settings as fateful and potentially dangerous. Thus, the respondents entered bars and bar settings with a generalized sense that there were reputational and physical safety risks associated with hanging out. However, participation in a violent confrontation led to a shift from a general to a specific concern about the risk of being assaulted:

    I: After this happened, did you avoid going to the bar?

Holt 1: No.

    I: In the first couple of days after this happened, were you concerned about what was going to happen when you saw this guy again?

Holt 1: We thought that we might see him again down at the bar and something might come out of it. . . . The only thing we were concerned about was, if we go back down there, he might have a few of his friends with him. Because he kept saying, "I'll go and get my friends."

Even when closure was established, respondents reported that they manifested specific changes in their routine orientation toward hanging out. A salient theme expressed was that once an individual had participated in a violent confrontation, he should always be alert and never trust his antagonist again:

> *I:* Did you do anything extra to protect yourself after this incident occurred?
>
> *Watson 1:* I became more alert. I never turn my back on nobody. Everything I do, everybody I see, I watch everybody. I don't underestimate anyone.

> *I:* So when you are on the scene—say, at Dot's, or you're just hanging out on State Street—and say they may be in the area, are you a little bit more sensitive to their presence?
>
> *Mac 3:* I always got my eye on them when they're around.
>
> *I:* And the reason that you have your eye on them is what?
>
> *Mac 3:* I don't trust them. I've seen them do really crazy things, especially when they're under the influence of alcohol, when they're drinking or getting high or something.

In addition to being in a state of alert, respondents' participation in violent confrontations altered how they viewed their relationships with their antagonists after closure of the incident:

> *I:* What is your relationship like now?
>
> *Mac 3:* Not as tight, and I don't trust them. But I don't dislike them.
>
> *I:* Why don't you trust them?
>
> *Mac 3:* Because I always feel that he wanted to do worse damage to me than he done.

> *I:* What is your relationship like with him at the present time? Is he hanging with you again?
>
> *Troy 3:* I don't play him too close.
>
> *I:* What does that mean?
>
> *Troy 3:* He be around, but I'm not going to treat him like I treated a man I be around every day.
>
> *I:* Can he come down to your crib?
>
> *Troy 3:* Can he come down to my crib? No, I already told him he can't.
>
> *I:* Before the Club George incident or after?
>
> *Troy 3:* I told him when he cut my jacket.
>
> *I:* You told him what?
>
> *Troy 3:* He can't come to the house.

Sequence of Events

A review of respondents' accounts of the sequence of events and interpersonal processes associated with the violent confrontations suggests that disrespectful actions that were defined as autonomy transgressions were the most important factor influencing their decision to resort to violence. For example, loud talking and "getting bad," insults and identity attacks, and unacceptable accounts emerged as significant catalysts for violence only after these actions had been negatively defined in light of standards associated with generalized normative expectations.

Three broad-ranging normative expectations or rules of behavior were observed, including "Respect other people," "Mind your own business," and "Avoid trouble." Respondents' accounts suggest that most of the incidents they described were precipitated by their antagonists, or by themselves engaging in behavior that violated one of the core normative expectations associated with hanging out in bars and bar settings.

Stage one of the sequence of events leading to violence began when one of the participants committed an overt or symbolic act that the other participant perceived as a potential threat to his manhood, physical safety, and/or reputation.

Stage two tended to involve a clarification process, in which the individual who thought that he or a relative or friend had been offended attempted to determine if he had accurately interpreted the intent and meaning of the antagonist's behavior. Stage two, therefore, involved an intra- and interpersonal process in which the offended participant sought to establish a valid definition of the situation. An important feature of this stage was an assessment of overt and symbolic cues associated with the antagonist's verbal statements and/or his physical actions.

Stage three involved the formulation of a plan of action and the actual physical confrontation. In situations in which the offended participant initiated violence, it occurred almost immediately after the antagonist failed to provide an acceptable account—that is, an excuse or justification for his behavior. In situations that were perceived as potentially violent, however, but that did not result in violence, stage three featured a de-escalation of the dispute as a result of a negotiated agreement to avoid a violent confrontation, one or both of the participants' lack of commitment to engaging in violence as a means of resolving the dispute, or successful third-party mediation.

Stage four of the sequence of events involved closure—that is, the termination or ending of conflict between individuals who have engaged in a potentially violent argument or an actual violent confrontation. Three types of closure were observed in respondents' accounts, including: symbolic, overt and internal.

Stage five of the sequence of events involved the aftermath or post-incident effects of violence participation. As we have seen, the termination of hostile verbal exchanges or physical violence does not automatically signal the end of a violent confrontation. Moreover, participation in a violent confrontation often led individuals to engage in a variety of psychological and behavioral adaptations to avoid being physically harmed by an antagonist at some other time or place following the initial violent confrontation.

The most significant factor influencing how individuals responded to their participation in a violent confrontation was closure. In situations in which respondents reported that closure had not been established, several post-incident effects were noted, including anticipation of additional acts of violence between respondents and their antagonists in the immediate future, packing a weapon, and changing routine activities associated with frequenting bars and bar settings.

The five stages described above represent the basic structure and interpersonal process associated with violent confrontations between black men in bars and bar settings. In addition to these stages, however, violent confrontations as interpersonal transactions and social events were also influenced by third parties. Third-party influences are discussed separately because third parties were able to contribute to the sequence of events during any of the five stages of interaction.

Third Parties

Due to the public nature of violent confrontations in bars and bar settings, third parties are often available to witness and influence their eventual outcome. A review of respondents' accounts provides evidence of three types of third parties, including mediators, instigators, and the instigating audience.

While respondents tended to express the view that they had made a personal decision to resort to violence, I uncovered significant direct and indirect evidence that suggested that various third parties, particularly members of the instigating audience, attempted to impose their definition of the situation and expectations on respondents and their antagonists, and that the respondents were aware of this at the time.

There was also a major contradiction regarding the respondents' accounts of whether their behavior or that of their antagonists was motivated by self-image concerns. Most respondents attributed their antagonists' verbal statements and physical actions to self-image-promotion concerns, motivated by a desire to look good in front of the crowd. However, respondents tended to deny that their own verbal statements and physical actions were motivated by similar self-image-promoting concerns. Rather, they chose to define their words and behavior as responses to normative violations that their antagonists had committed, and they therefore explicitly described themselves as norm enforcers. Other evidence, however, suggest that respondents' verbal statements and physical actions were also motivated by self-image concerns, particularly self-image-defending and reputation-defending concerns. Specific evidence that supports this conclusion is respondents' references to the attempts of the instigating audience to impose its definition of the situation on the violent participants, and the reputational implications associated with unsuccessful management of interpersonal conflict in bars and bar settings.

Conclusion

The findings reported above are significant because they describe critical stages in the sequence of events leading to nonfatal violence among black men. These findings may also be used to enhance knowledge of what Luck-enbill refers to as "the historical roots" of criminal homicide.[5] That is, the sequence of events and definition of situations leading to nonfatal violence may in some cases function as rehearsals for encounters that result in fatal violence at some other time or place.

In the next chapter, the validity of the four hypotheses that the study was designed to test are assessed in terms of the findings derived from respondents' accounts. The relevance of the findings to previous research related to violence as an interpersonal process will also be discussed.

8
DISCUSSION OF FINDINGS

This study made it possible to test the validity of four hypotheses derived from a theoretical perspective based on the literature relating to interpersonal dynamics of violent confrontations between black men. In this chapter, I examine the findings in light of the research hypotheses in Chapter 4.

Validity of Hypotheses

Hypothesis 1

In Hypothesis 1, I predicted that

> Violent confrontations between black males in bar and bar settings are generally precipitated by one or both combatants' interpretation of the other as engaging in rule-violating behavior associated with the expression of compulsive masculinity.

Findings reported in Chapter 6 and 7 provide some convincing evidence to support Hypothesis 1. In Chapter 6, for example, I summarized the respondents' descriptions of rules of conduct that they felt had been established to regulate interpersonal relations between black men and factors that they believed contribute to violent confrontations. When I asked respondents to explain what causes violent confrontations between black men, they most often listed drug-trafficking and trying to "get over," women and romantic competition, and disrespect. A comparison of these factors with the descriptive categories listed in the Compulsive Masculinity Index suggests that respondents tended to explain the causes of violent confrontations between black men with reference to behavior associated with compulsive masculinity. For example, disputes related to drug-trafficking and trying to "get over" represent references to the manipulation norm. The specific features of this norm include an emphasis on the exploitation of others through the use of one's wits.

Respondents who listed drug-trafficking and trying to "get over" as causes of violence among black men expressed the view that in incidents precipitated by manipulation, violence occurs as a retributive reaction to mitigate or punish an individual for attempting to exploit someone else. In addition, some respondents expressed the view that violence might occur as a preemptive stance, to protect oneself from being disrespected or assaulted by the individual one has attempted to exploit.

References to women and romantic competitiion as a cause of violence among black men are consistent with the sexual conquest descriptive category. The Compulsive Masculinity Index defines sexual conquest as a norm in which manhood is defined in terms of sexual conquest and emotional and financial exploitation of females. Respondents who listed women and romantic competition as a cause of violence expressed the view that the catalyst for violence in these situations often involved jealousy motivated by losing a romantic competition and/or awareness of a wife or girlfriend's sexual infidelity.

The content and meanings that respondents attributed to disrespect as a cause of violence suggest that such disrespect tended to include references to both autonomy and toughness norms. For example, in explaining how disrespect contributes to violent confrontations, respondents described what they considered to be a typical situation in which an antagonist might violate another man's autonomy by loud talking or directing insults or identity attacks against him or attempting to impose his definition of order in a situation.

In addition, some respondents believed that there are black men who may precipitate violence by engaging in toughness displays as a means of projecting unqualified autonomy or claiming superiority. That is, they seek to communicate to others through various toughness displays that they can and will do whatever they want to do and are immune to the orders and instructions of others. Consequently, violence occurs as an attempt by the man who perceives himself as disrespected to defend himself against what is ultimately defined as an autonomy transgression.

While Chapter 6 provided descriptions of how respondents defined and made sense out of routine activities and their perspectives on the causes of violent confrontations between black men who frequent bars and bar settings, the focus of Chapter 7 was on how respondents interpreted the causes and dynamics of violent confrontations in which they were major participants.

The findings discussed in Chapter 7 suggest that respondents were un-equivocal in their description and definition of their antagonists' actions as constituting rule-violating behavior associated with the expression of the toughness norm of compulsive masculinity. For example, most of the inci-dents that they related were precipitated by loud talking and "getting bad," insults and identity attacks, and disrespect and unacceptable accounts. Eval-uation of these causes or precipitating events in accordance with the descrip-tive categories listed in the Compulsive Masculinity Index suggest that the respondents tended to define their antagonists' intentions and behaviors as indications of their commitment to the toughness norm.

However, these findings do not directly support Hypothesis 1 with re-gard to how respondents defined their own intentions and behavior. The respondents often described their antagonists as engaging in behavior involv-ing the projection of toughness. But they tended to describe their own in-tentions and actions as attempts to defend themselves, to defend a relative or friend, or to punish an antagonist for committing a rule violation, such as demonstrating disrespect and/or a willingness to engage in violence against the respondent or a relative or friend of the respondent. Thus, most of the respondents defined themselves as norm enforcers. This observation is con-sistent with Toch's definition of norm enforcing as "a self-assigned mission involving the use of violence on behalf of norms that the violent person sees as universal rules of conduct."[1]

Examination of the accounts did not uncover a significant number of direct references to a concern with projecting a "tough guy" image, as a factor motivating respondents to engage in violence against their antagonists. However, the respondents felt that they consistently manifested an overt concern with protecting and projecting their autonomy.

The Compulsive Masculinity Index defines autonomy as a norm that defines manhood in terms of immunity to the orders and instructions of others. Many of the accounts that the respondents provided included refer-ences to autonomy concerns. Their decision to use violence typically in-volved a definition of the antagonist's actions—such as loud talking and "getting bad," insults and identity attacks, and disrespect and unacceptable accounts—as representing an autonomy transgression. Thus, the respondents tended to justify their use of violence against their antagonists as an attempt to mitigate the adverse social and personal consequences of being a victim of an autonomy transgression.

Moreover, these self-characterizations project a self-image in which au-tonomy concerns are more important to the respondents in constructing their identity as men than defining themselves as "tough." Indeed, it is ironic that those lower-class black men who are least likely to participate in mainstream institutions and activities and who are the most socially impotent men in America appear to be overtly concerned with presenting themselves as free from external interference.

In sum, the findings derived from this study support the basic predictions of Hypothesis 1. However, the respondents relied on references to different aspects of the compulsive masculinity alternative to explain the intentions and behavior of their antagonists and themselves. For example, the respondents perceived their antagonists as engaging in behavior indicative of a commitment to the toughness norm. But they regarded their own behavior as motivated by a desire to protect their autonomy.

While the respondents provided very few accounts that would suggest that their behavior was primarily motivated by a desire to project and/or promote a "tough guy" image, there is evidence that respondents did engage in behavior that subserved the toughness norm. For example, respondents often employed overt displays of toughness, such as loud talking or assaulting their antagonist, to accomplish what they described as protecting their autonomy.

Finally, as I have noted, when I asked the respondents what generally causes violent confrontations to occur between black men in bars and bar settings, they most frequently listed disputes precipitated by drug-trafficking and trying to "get over," women and romantic competition, and disrespect. However, when they were asked to list the causes of violent confrontations in which they were one of the primary participants, they tended to list loud talking and "getting bad," insults and identity attacks, and disrespect and unacceptable accounts. The differences in the two listings reflect the respondents' efforts to make qualitative distinctions between objective causes of typical incidents and subjective interpretations of their antagonists' intentions and behavior. Thus, the respondents emphasized an objective reason for conflict when asked to describe the causes of typical incidents. However, when they were asked to describe the causes of specific incidents in which they had been a participant, they emphasized subjective interpretations of their antagonists' behavior. That is, they emphasized intra- and interpersonal processes that culminated in violence.

Hypothesis 2

In Hypothesis 2, I predicted that

> The occurrence of interpersonal conflict between black males while frequenting bars and bar settings often leads to face-saving concerns and actions due to the presence of third parties.

Several respondents reported that their actions were motivated by a desire to "look good" or project a positive presentation of self before persons who witnessed the dispute between themselves and their antagonists. The majority of respondents reported, however, that their actions were not motivated by a desire to look good. Thus, the accounts provide very little direct evidence to support Hypothesis 2 in terms of how respondents interpreted their own motivations and behavior. That is, examination of the literal or surface meanings of responses to questions constructed to tap face-saving or self-image concerns indicates that the majority of respondents did not regard their motivations or behavior as being influenced by a desire to look good in front of various third parties. Rather than being concerned with how others evaluated their management of a dispute, respondents generally reported that they were primarily concerned with monitoring their antagonists' verbal and nonverbal cues in order to avoid being hit or physically harmed.

While I found very little self-descriptive evidence to support Hypothesis 2 regarding how respondents interpreted their motivations and behavior, I did uncover substantial evidence to support the hypothesis in terms of how respondents defined the motivations and behavior *of their antagonists*. Most of the respondents expressed the view, for example, that their antagonists were concerned about looking good in front of various third parties who witnessed the dispute. Specific evidence they offered to demonstrate their antagonists' concerns with looking good, included references to the antagonists deliberately and self-consciously engaging in loud talking, directing insults against the respondent, and/or initiating violence by threatening the respondent or actually committing a violent act.

Divergent responses to questions constructed to tap face-saving and self-image concerns may reflect a lack of precision in the formulation of Hypothesis 2 and the various questions and probes I used to acquire an understanding of the respondents' perception of this aspect of the violence process. For example, I regarded the questions "Were you trying to look good?" and "Did he do anything that made you think he was concerned about looking good in front of the crowd?" as constructed to tap a variety of issues related to face-saving or self-image concerns. The respondents, however, tended to interpret these questions as asking whether they or their antagonists engaged in speech or other acts indicative of a concern with self-image-promoting.

In his empirically based typology of violent men, Toch defines *self-image-promoting* as "The use of violence as a demonstration of worth, by persons whose self-definition places emphasis on toughness and status."[2] In addition to describing their antagonists' use of violence as influenced by self-image-promoting concerns, the respondents tended to regard their antagonists' speech and behavior preceding the occurrence of violence as motivated by self-image-promoting concerns.

Characterizing their antagonists as self-image-promoters is consistent with the respondents' definition of themselves as norm enforcers—that is, as individuals who resort to "the use of violence on behalf of norms that the violent person sees as universal rules of conduct." The counterpart characterization of their antagonists as self-image-promoters is logical and expected when evaluated against a broader consideration of the findings. However, the self-characterizations must be viewed with caution. For example, many of the respondents did engage in loud talking, insult their antagonists, threaten their antagonists, and/or initiate the first acts of violence. Therefore, based on my review and interpretation of the findings, I am not convinced that the respondents engaged in these behaviors *only* to deter or punish antagonists for committing various rule violations and were not motivated by face-saving or self-image concerns. I was able to uncover significant indirect evidence that supports the validity of Hypothesis 2 with regard to the respondents' motivations and that suggests that their behavior was influenced by face-saving and self-image concerns.

In the respondents' accounts of the contributions of third parties, for example, bystanders often encouraged one or both participants to resort to violence to resolve disputes. I introduced the term *instigating audience* to denote this group of third parties. Findings that document the existence of an instigating audience are significant because they suggest that lower-class black men regard violent confrontations in bars and bar settings as participatory events, in which persons other than the combatants contribute to how these incidents are defined and to their eventual outcome.

Finally, findings that an instigating audience may constrain a dispute toward a violent confrontation represents indirect evidence that supports Hypothesis 2. That is, the respondents reported that they were very aware of the presence of a chorus of pro-violence bystanders who wanted to see a fight. Given these additional observations, therefore, it is not plausible that respondents were at once aware of an instigating audience and at the same time totally immune to their encouragement of violence and other definitions of the situation.

Findings on how respondents justified their use of violence against their antagonists provides additional indirect evidence supporting Hypothesis 2. Respondents generally believed that how an individual performed in a violent confrontation had reputational implications. Moreover, they reported that resorting to violence was often necessary in order to deter others from attempting to take advantage of them in the future.

Surely men aware of the post-incident reputational implications of violence participation are going to be influenced by face-saving and self-image concerns at least to a certain extent as a socially significant event is unfolding. True, face-saving and self-image concerns may not be one's most salient concerns when confronted with the immediate possibility of incurring a physical injury. Given the cultural context described by the respondents, however, it is implausible that face-saving and self-image concerns would be excluded in conflict-ridden situations. The responses suggest that questions like "Were you trying to look good?" were not the best way to uncover direct indications of face-saving or self-image concerns. However, the indirect evidence that the respondents' motivations and behavior were influenced by face-saving and self-image concerns is substantial and convincing.

The respondents' accounts of how third parties, particularly the instigating audience, contributed to violent confrontations in which they participated suggest that in addition to being influenced by a desire to enforce norms, some of the respondents resorted to violence as a means of self-image-defending. Toch defines *self-image-defending* as violence engaged in by individuals who have "a tendency to use aggression as a form of retribution against people who the person feels have cast aspersions on his self-image."[3]

Self-image-defending concerns were particularly salient in incidents in which respondents claimed that their antagonists precipitated the confrontation by directing insults, threats, or identity attacks against them. Moreover, autonomy transgressions committed in the presence of third parties tended to lead to a surfacing of audience-directed self-image-defending concerns.

Hypothesis 3

In Hypothesis 3, I predicted that

> Given the public visibility of violent confrontations that occur in bars and bar settings, third parties often influence the outcome of these encounters.

All the incidents that respondents provided occurred in the presence of third parties. The public visibility of these incidents was related to the subject of the study and to its specific emphasis on obtaining accounts of violent confrontations that occurred in bars, in after-hours joints, in poolrooms, or on street corners—that is, in social settings which are heavily patronized by lower-class black men.

Third parties who witnessed violent confrontations were described by respondents as mediators, instigators, or members of the instigating audience. However, the respondents' accounts provide only partial support for the prediction that "third parties often influence the outcome of these encounters." Many respondents, for example, described how various third parties attempted to mediate or instigate disputes between themselves and their antagonists. But the respondents tended to make a distinction between third parties attempting to impose their definitions of the situation on one or both of the participants and their personal decision on whether they should resort to violence. In several accounts, mediators failed in their efforts to deter the respondents from resorting to violence. The respondents' decision to resort to violence in these situations was generally motivated by anger and an intense desire to punish an antagonist for committing an inexcusable rule violation.

Several respondents provided accounts of incidents in which they resisted the encouragement of instigators or members of the instigating audience to shift the encounter from an argumentative verbal exchange to a violent confrontation. Respondents who mentioned this pattern of resistance to third-party influence reported that they were aware of the instigators' call to violence but decided to resist their encouragement in favor of a juncture when they determined it would be either normatively or strategically appropriate for them to escalate the conflict.

Regarding the validity of Hypothesis 3, the respondents' accounts did not support the existence of a direct relationship between third-party intervention and the final outcome of a dispute. What the findings do suggest is that various third parties often attempt to influence the outcome of these encounters by expressing their views or definitions of the situation and that violence participants prefer to perceive themselves as self-consciously determining whether they should resort to violence is a given situation.

While most respondents expressed the view that they were solely responsible for their decision to resort to violence, some indirect evidence suggested that third parties do influence the final outcome of disputes that occur in bars and bar settings.

The instigating audience was the spectator group that respondents most often cited in their accounts of how third parties attempted to influence the outcome of a dispute. Descriptions of the contributions of the instigating audience frequently included references to normative expectations and a variety of self-image and reputational concerns. Thus, many respondents expressed the view that in disputes between black men, the instigating audience is not only interested in imposing its definition of the situation but seeks to establish a deterministic context that would constrain the dispute toward a violent confrontation.

Hypothesis 4

In Hypothesis 4, I predicted that

> Involvement in a violent confrontation in a bar or bar setting leads many black males to alter routine activities associated with frequenting bars and bar settings.

The findings suggest that the validity of Hypothesis 4 as a predictive statement is limited because it failed to anticipate the range of post-incident effects associated with violent confrontations between black males in bars and bar settings. For example, a major shortcoming of Hypothesis 4 is its lack of emphasis on making a distinction between changes in routine orientations and routine patterns of behavior. Respondents provided numerous accounts of how they changed their psychological orientation (such as "anticipating violence," "being alert," "never trusting their antagonist again"). Moreover, respondents tended to report that changes in routine orientations toward hanging out in bars and bar settings were more common than changing or altering routine activities.

The findings do suggest, however, that some respondents changed their routine activities associated with frequenting bars and bar settings subsequent to participating in a violent confrontation. Several factors contributed to their decisions to change routine activities. First, the perception that conflict closure had not been established led some individuals to avoid bars and bar settings, because they anticipated additional acts of violence between themselves and their antagonists. This finding illustrates a link between the definition of the situation, the emergence of a change in routine orientation, and a subsequent change in one's routine activities.

Second, some respondents deliberately avoided bars and bar settings following their participation in a violent confrontation in order to end the confrontation between themselves and their antagonists. That is, by avoiding bars and bar settings, they sought to symbolically communicate to their antagonists that the incident was over.

Third, respondents who had suffered serious physical injuries tended to report that they had changed their routine activities in order to heal and regain their health.

Finally, several respondents reported that they had been forced to change their routine activities after they were imprisoned for the acts of violence that they had committed against their antagonists.

These findings suggest that involvement in a violent confrontation in a bar or bar setting does not automatically translate into overt changes in routine activities associated with frequenting bars and bar settings. Thus, the predictive validity of Hypothesis 4 is limited to situations involving specific definitions of the situation and circumstances.

Relevance of Findings to Existing Research

Autonomy Concerns and Violence

One of the most significant findings uncovered in this study is that violent confrontations between lower-class black men are often precipitated by verbal statements or behaviors that are defined as autonomy transgressions. In his ethnographic study of lower-class blacks residing in Washington, D.C., Hannerz found a similar association. For example, Hannerz reports:

> it seems that most of the violence which occurs has the form of brawls following arguments. Meddling, scorn, and condescending manner come into conflict with the men's feeling for autonomy. "He's a man and I'm a man, and, I don't take no shit like that," is how streetcorner men tend to defend or explain their fighting responses.[4]

The observation that an autonomy transgression is a major factor contributing to violent confrontations between lower-class black men is also consistent with Horowitz's findings regarding the association between dishonor and violence among Chicano men. According to Horowitz, Chicano men tend to justify the use of violence against others by using a honor/dishonor standard to evaluate each other's conduct and to define their personal sense of masculine integrity.

In the Chicano cultural context, *honor* refers to "a person's ability to command deference in interpersonal relations." Consequently, Horowitz found, violent confrontations involving Chicano men were frequently precipitated by acts defined as carrying implications of dishonor. That is, the acts were challenges to honor that men could not ignore, lest they be perceived as possessing character attributes suggesting "a failure of manliness or the physical capacity to maintain claims to precedence among peers."[5]

The honor tradition is a deeply entrenched feature of Hispanic culture. It exerts substantial influence on definitions of self, presentation of self in public settings, and interpersonal relations. While the honor tradition is not a deeply entrenched feature of lower-class black culture, particularly in terms of how black men define gender-specific roles and duties toward women and family members, ethnographic studies of inner-city blacks suggest that black men attach a great deal of importance to projecting and enacting a masculine role-orientation that emphasizes autonomy from external interference. Indeed, the findings reported in Chapter 7 provide convincing evidence that perceived threats to autonomy function as a major catalyst and justification for violence participation among black men in bars and bar settings.

Reciprocity and Violence

In addition to being influenced by cultural traditions associated with the expression of various masculinity role orientations—such as the "tough guy" image, the "player of women" image, the thrill-seeker, the hustler, and the like—the findings of this study suggest that autonomy concerns that lead to violent confrontations between black men may also involve a lack of reciprocity in interpersonal relations.

A *reciprocal relationship* is a social interaction in which there exists a constant process of giving and receiving. According to Gouldner, reciprocity is a universal moral norm that contributes to the stability of social systems. To demonstrate a lack of reciprocity by committing deliberate acts of unreciprocal behavior is a major source of tension and interpersonal conflict that may lead to violence.[6]

I found that insults, identity attacks, and refusing to provide an acceptable account of one's behavior were often defined as autonomy transgressions in situations that resulted in violence between black men. Thus, the findings in this study support Palmer's theoretical assertions regarding the association between masculine identity threats—that is, unreciprocal acts—and violent confrontations between black men. According to Palmer,

> It is the unreciprocating slights of his masculinity that so often trigger violence. Any disparagement of masculinity is cause for the male to aggress, especially if he is of the lower class and black. . . . When it appears to him that one or more threaten through unreciprocity to destroy whatever fragile identity he possesses, he takes violent action against them.[7]

Many of the men I interviewed described insults, identity attacks, and unacceptable accounts that they had experienced as unreciprocating in that they perceived these actions as patronizing and incompatible with concepts of manhood.

Definitions of the Situation

Awareness of generalized normative expectations is responsible for the emergence of definitions of the situation that lead to various patterns of behavior, including interpersonal violence. Hewitt has defined the term *definition of the situation* as "referring to an organization of perception, in which people assemble objects, meanings, and others in social space and time and act toward them in a coherent, organized way."[8] Defining situations is an important feature of human interaction because it helps individuals identify their roles and the roles of others with whom they are interacting at any given time. Motives or accepted justifications for present, future, or past acts evolve as a result of some definition of actions, behavior, or circumstances against a cultural framework or body of normative expectations. For example, Stokes and Hewitt have suggested that "problematic situations often involve misalignment between the actual or intended acts of participants and cultural ideals, expectations, beliefs, knowledge and the like."[9]

Findings reported in Chapter 6 and 7 support the theoretical assertion of Mills, Hewitt, and Stokes and Hewitt regarding the relationship between normative expectations, definitions of the situation, and behavior. For example, the most common justification for resorting to violence given by the men I interviewed was that an antagonist, in their view, had deliberately violated the rules of "Mind your own business" and "Avoid trouble," by engaging in actions that constituted disrespect.

Motives are another important feature of the process in which normative expectations and definitions of the situation converge and lead to interpersonal violence. Symbolic interactionists generally distinguish between *motivation* and *motive*. *Motivation* generally refers to an internal state that governs impulsive responses to various stimuli, while a *motive* is a statement that a person makes about his or her own conduct or the conduct of others.

Some findings reported above suggest that definitions of the situation leading to violent confrontations may also function as a motive state: that is, circumstances in which an individual evaluates a particular situation, attributes meaning to the situation, considers a variety of responses, and decides on a particular course of action.

The findings also suggest that definitions of situations leading to violence are not static, but dynamic. The precipitating event in most of the incidents, for example, was defined as a rule violation that required some type of norm enforcement in response. However, in incidents in which an antagonist refused to provide an acceptable account of his allegedly offensive actions toward the respondents' relative or friend, the definition of the situation was nearly always expanded to include disrespect of the respondent as another source of conflict. Moreover, expansion of the definition of the situation often personalized the conflict for respondents who had initially intervened in a situation as norm enforcers and subsequently felt themselves involved in a situation in which their self-image or reputation was at risk of being adversely affected.

Justifying Violence

In their theory, "techniques of neutralization," Sykes and Matza have suggested that a distinct set of justifications exists that individuals adopt in order to justify violations of mainstream social norms. The specific techniques of neutralization they describe include denial of responsibility, denial of injury, denial of victim, condemnation of condemner, and appeal to higher loyalties.[10]

One of the major goals of this study was to gain insight into how black men justify their participation in violent incidents. Findings reported in Chapter 7 suggest that *denial of victim* was a consistently salient theme in respondents' accounts. According to Sykes and Matza, denial of victim is a neutralization technique in which the offender justifies his delinquent or criminal behavior by defining it as "a form of rightful retaliation or punishment." In addition, the offender regards the antagonist not as a victim but as a person who deserves injury or punishment.

Respondents' references to justifications involving denial of victim are also consistent with Black's discussion of expressive violence as a form of self-help.[11] For example, most of the respondents justified their resort to violence as a means of pursuing justice in a situation in which an antagonist had violated a subculturally relevant rule or social norm.

A second major neutralization technique that the respondents used in their accouts is *the appeal to higher loyalties*. According to Sykes and Matza, "deviation from certain norms may occur not because the norms are rejected but because other norms, held to be more pressing or involving a higher loyalty, are accorded precedence."[12] Appeals to higher loyalties were a salient theme in respondents' accounts of violent incidents involving their defense of a relative or friend. However, the findings also suggest that in encounters precipitated by attempts to defend a relative or friend, respondents also invoked denial of victim as a justification for resorting to violence. References to denial of victim tended to emerge when respondents described specific stages in an encounter in which they had personalized insults or other unacceptable behavior that an antagonist directed against them after their attempts to intervene and mediate a pre-existing conflict that occurred between the antagonist and a relative or friend of the respondent.

Findings reported in Chapter 7 do not provide empirical support for the respondents' use of neutralization techniques as pre-incident justifications that allow them to resort to violence as a means of resolving interpersonal conflict. What the findings do validate is that violent black men often use denial of victim and appeals to higher loyalties as post-incident justifications to make sense of and to explain their own participation in violent incidents in bars and bar settings.

Violence as an Interpersonal Process

Findings reported in Chapter 7 support existing thinking and empirical research that suggests that the most important factor leading to interpersonal violence is the perception that some type of identity threat has been committed. For example, the findings are very consistent with Hepburn's explanation of the sequence of events leading to violent behavior in interpersonal relationships.[13] According to Hepburn, violent confrontations are generally precipitated by a two-stage process. Stage one involves an individual's perception that his identity has been threatened. Stage two includes the formulation of a retaliatory tactic for reducing the identity threat.

Accounts by the men I interviewed suggest an interpersonal process that is nearly identical to the one described by Hepburn. For example, I found that most of the incidents began with a stage one in which a respondent perceived his antagonist as having committed an act that represented a potential threat to his manhood, physical safety, and/or reputation.

In stage two, respondents tended to engage in a clarification attempt in order to determine their antagonist's intent. Finally in stage three respondents tended to formulate a plan of action. This process is similar to Hepburn's model. The interpersonal process that I uncovered, however, also included an effort by respondents to confirm their definition of the situation. Hepburn's model fails to consider how individuals attempt to validate the intent of others.

The findings reported in Chapter 7 also provide evidence that supports Hepburn's observation that identity threats alone are not enough to precipitate a violent confrontation and that there are five intervening factors that must impact on the situation. These factors include adherence to norms that condone violence, experience or successful use of violence in the past, a predisposition to engage in argumentative behavior while under the influence of alcohol or drugs, the presence of third parties who may provide implicit or explicit support for face-saving tactics that lead to violence, and a perception that acceptance or avoidance would impose too high a cost with respect to the maintenance of a positive identity.

Regarding norms that condone violence, respondents reported that there were three rules of the street that often lead to violence if they are violated. These rules include "Respect other people," "Mind your own business," and "Avoid trouble." References to how they or their antagonists violated one or all of these "rules of the street" was a salient theme in respondent's accounts.

The experience or successful use of violence in the past was a significant factor in how some of the men I interviewed calculated their participation in violent confrontations. References to experience or successful use of violence in the past were primarily limited to the accounts of the more prolific violent men. Their references to past incidents tended to focus on how they had generally managed interpersonal conflict and closure.

Regarding a predisposition to engage in argumentative behavior while under the influence of alcohol or drugs, many of the men believed that alcohol or drug consumption had contributed to how they responded to identity threats and other rule violations committed against them by their antagonists. However, when asked to justify their use of violence in a particular incident, most respondents downplayed the influence of pre-incident alcohol or drug use and tended to refer to how they became angered and wanted to punish their antagonist for committing certain rule violations.

The findings provide support for Hepburn's observation that "the presence of third parties may provide implicit or explicit support for face-saving tactics that lead to violence." The contribution and influence of the instigating audience is a prime example of the effect that third parties have on violent confrontations.

Finally, the findings reported in Chapter 7 provide strong support for Hepburn's observation that the decision to engage in violence to resolve a dispute is often influenced by "a perception that acceptance or avoidance would impose a high cost with respect to the maintenance of a positive identity."[14]

The three-stage process that I observed in the respondents' accounts is also consistent with the empirically derived three-stage sequence of events described by Felson and Steadman.[15] However, while the three-stage sequence of events described by Felson and Steadman is strictly behavioral, the three-stage sequence of events that I described includes both behavioral and cognitive processes.

Luckenbill and Levi have found evidence that suggested to them that participants involved in violent confrontations tend to establish a working agreement that the situation is suited for violence.[16] In stage two of the sequence of events, I found that the offended participants would attempt to clarify the intent of their antagonists. Respondents often assumed a working agreement to engage in violence was established when their antagonist failed to provide an acceptable account of his behavior, insulted or threatened the identity of the respondent, or physically assaulted the respondent. However, it should be noted that in many incidents a mutually defined working agreement to engage in violence was not explicit. Rather, the working agreement to resort to violence was often a product of how one of the participants defined the overt or symbolic acts of his antagonist.

While Athens has dismissed the significance of character contests as a primary motivation for most acts of criminal violence, he does allow for the possibility of character contests as a feature of "an extremely limited subclass of purely assaultive violent criminals acts which closely approximate duels of a much earlier era."[17] The findings of this study affirm Athens' views regarding character contests as a feature of specific types of violent encounters. More specifically, the findings reported above strongly suggest that violent confrontations motivated by character contests tend to be population and situation specific. Defense of character or self-image, for example, are major concerns of black men who participate in violent confrontations in bars and bar settings. The social importance of bars and bar setting as stages upon which black men attempt to demonstrate commitment to compulsive masculinity increases the likelihood that these individuals will be overtly sensitive to the reputational implications associated with failure to adequately respond to efforts by an antagonist to cast aspersions on one's character.

Rule Violations, Identity Threats, and the Emotive Aspects of Violence

A vigorous debate over motivation for violence is currently being waged among violence researchers. Some attribute violent incidents to norms that condone violence as an acceptable means of resolving disputes or as an attempt to defend one's character against identity attacks. Others attribute motivation to angry outbursts and a desire to punish an antagonist for committing a harmful act.

The findings presented in this study suggest that this debate may impose an artificial distinction on the violence process. That is, in a scramble to attribute violent actions to a single motive, many violence researchers have failed to consider the fact that violence is carried out for many reasons. Interactions leading to violence are dynamic, and motives may change or be rearranged in terms of their priority as the transaction unfolds. Berkowitz and Katz have presented findings that strongly suggest that emotions such as anger, humiliation, righteousness and rage often facilitate the resort to lethal violence.[18] However, the accounts of the men I interviewed suggest that violence-provoking emotions (such as anger, humiliation, and rage) do not emerge in a social vacuum independent from normative considerations. In justifying their willingness to resort to violence, the respondents specifically characterized injurious acts committed against them or their relatives or friends as rule violations that warranted a punitive response. According to Duncan, we do not know shame, envy, pride, or disgust at birth.[19] Rather, "we learn these social feelings in communication with others whose response teaches us what our acts mean to them and thus to ourselves, as we play our roles in the community."

With respect to the emotive basis of violent confrontations involving black males in bars and bar settings, my findings support Katz's findings on the role of humiliation in transactions that culminate in violence.[20] For example, Katz claims that violent incidents are often precipitated by identity challenges or acts that are perceived as degrading, subsequently resulting in the emergence of humiliating feelings. According to Katz, "within humiliation, there is a profound apprehension of the power of others to control one's soul."[21] This definition of the personal impact of experiencing humiliation is similar to what my respondents described as autonomy transgressions. The emotive basis of their attempts to protect themselves against autonomy transgressions involved concerns about avoiding humiliation. Not responding to an autonomy transgression would represent, in Katz's terminology, "successful scarification," or in the vocabulary of my respondents, possibly being branded a "punk" or "chump."

Moreover, my findings support Katz with regard to designating violent transactions as moral battles in which some individuals are motivated to violence by a righteous anger in pursuit of a righteous punishment of the wrongdoer.

Research and Findings on Violence in Bars

Research on barroom violence is limited and has failed to provide an adequate examination of the interpersonal dynamics of violent confrontations between bar patrons. However, the existing research suggests that barroom violence typically involves participants who are young, male, low-income, and under the influence of alcohol.

In his study of violence in English pubs, based on interviews with bar owners and bartenders, Marsh found that barroom violence was often precipitated when men deliberately attempted to use the bar setting to enhance their status by retaliating against those who they believed had cast aspersions on their honor or reputation. While the findings reported in Chapter 7 describe status concerns, they do not suggest that most of the respondents felt that they engage in violence in order to enhance or promote their self-image. Instead, respondents reported that they were primarily concerned with defending and preserving a socially acceptable manhood image. Accounts in which respondents reported being motivated by a desire to enhance or promote their self-image were rare. Respondents who were prolific fighters were most likely to report that their actions were motivated by a desire to enhance their self-image or reputation in the community. In some cases, however, respondents expressed the view that a credible defense of status could have significant reputational implications regarding how they were perceived in the community.

Research on violence in bars has also found that bars provide a social setting in which individuals who are most likely to engage in violent behavior may interact with each other.[22] The findings reported in Chapter 7 support this observation. For example, many of the respondents' routine activities centered on hanging out to socialize, to sell, purchase, or use drugs, to meet women, and to manipulate or exploit others. Consequently, these routine activities frequently contributed to interpersonal conflict resulting in a violent confrontation.

In the final chapter, a brief discussion of the prevention and research implications of the findings of this study will be provided.

9

RESEARCH AND PREVENTION IMPLICATIONS

Research

The findings reported in Chapters 6 and 7 offer positive support for criminological theories that suggest that the high rates of interpersonal violence among blacks is influenced by their adherence to values and norms that condone violence as a legitimate means to resolve interpersonal conflict. Comparative studies of the interpersonal dynamics of violent confrontations are needed in order to determine whether the precipitating events, definitions of situation, justification for violence, and post-incident effects observed in the accounts of black men are similar or dissimilar to interpersonal processes associated with violent confrontations among white, Hispanic, or Asian men.

The findings reported here also suggest the need to extend Levi's work by directing more attention to how the relationship of violent participants influences the sequence of events, particularly definitions of the situation and the contribution of third parties.

To move forward with the development of the integrated theoretical perspective as an empirically valid explanation, several factors should be considered in designing studies to test the theory.

To conceptualize and operationalize the "player of women" and "tough guy" images, attitudinal data on a cross-section of black males must be collected to develop an index that would measure the extent to which black males adhere to these roles. Moreover, "player of women" and "tough guy" indexes would be useful as methodological devices for conducting content analysis of the personal accounts of black violent offenders and victims. That is, such indexes could help researchers interested in examining the interpersonal dynamics of black-on-black violence to make distinctions between violent incidents precipitated by adherence to dysfunctional definitions of manhood and those precipitated by instrumental issues or concerns (such as drug-trafficking, disputes, robberies, and rapes).

Second, because of higher rates of nonfatal interpersonal violence (like assault, aggravated assault, rape, and robbery) than of fatal violence, more studies that examine the situational determinants, phenomenological meanings, and interpersonal processes associated with nonfatal violence among blacks are needed. Few studies of this aspect of black-on-black violence exist, yet we know that many of the incidents that result in fatal violence are preceded by incidents involving nonfatal violence. Studies of nonfatal violence among blacks therefore have the potential of making a significant contribution to our understanding of the intrapersonal and interpersonal processes leading to black-on-black homicide. Moreover, studies of this type could provide added data that can be used to assess the explanatory power of the integrated theoretical perspective and other theoretical explanations of black-on-black violence.

Prevention Implications

Interpersonal violence among black men is a product of multiple causes, and therefore multiple solutions are required to reduce its rate of occurrence. Many observers have argued that a broad coalition should be established between federal and state governments, the private sector, the educational system, and locally based community centers to reduce those factors such as school drop-out, unemployment, and substance abuse that lead a disproportionate number of lower-income men to spend an inordinate amount of time in bars and bar settings.[1] A strong argument for the multiple-solution agenda has been developed by the Eisenhower Foundation to reduce crime and other social problems among inner-city residents.[2]

The specific recommendations of the Eisenhower Foundation include:

1. Early intervention and urban school reform
2. Establishment of a youth investment corporation
3. Reforming existing school-to-work transition programs
4. A community enterprise development strategy for the inner city
5. Increased funding for drug abuse prevention and treatment

Although implementing liberal structural reforms such as those recommended by Currie, Curtis, the Eisenhower Foundation, and Wilson are important,[3] the findings of this study suggest that structural reforms alone will not reduce the high rates of interpersonal violence among black males. I agree with Newman that what liberals and social scientists have failed to consider about the etiology of interpersonal violence in that it is not a unitary phenomenon precipitated by a direct causal association between racial discrimination, income inequality, unemployment, and violence. Rather, assault and homicide are interpersonal transactions that occur in specific situational and social contexts.[4]

The findings presented in this study are context-specific and strongly suggest that in addition to structural reforms there is an immediate need for prevention strategies specifically targeted toward reforming the social context in which black males internalize values and norms that lead to the adoption of compulsive masculinity role orientations and lifestyles that increase their likelihood of becoming involved in disputes that culminate in violence. Therefore, reduction of interpersonal violence among black males requires a prevention agenda that attempts to modify the social context in which black males at risk for becoming involved in violent incidents interact. Reform of the social context must include community-based coalitions to prevent violence, black male schools or classrooms, mentoring and manhood development programs, multicomponent community centers, and community policing.

Community-Based Coalitions to Prevent Violence

Such coalitions should be established to create and coordinate violence-prevention programs in high-risk neighborhoods. Among the specific programs I would recommend are weekly neighborhood marches and rallies in areas where black males hang out—that is, bars, major street corners, parking lots, crack houses, and so on. The primary purpose of these marches and rallies would be to increase community awareness of the violence problem, encourage concerned members of the community to become involved in organized efforts to prevent violence, and make those males who engage in at-risk behavior aware that violence is an unacceptable means of resolving conflict.

Community-based coalitions should also work with local politicians, religious and business leaders, and community groups to establish recreational, tutorial, conflict-resolution, and vocational training programs. Moreover, volunteers should be encouraged to implement these programs, as the reduction of violence among black men must emphasize community ownership of the violence problem and self-help.

Black Male Classrooms or Schools

Black male schools and classrooms should be established in at-risk communities in order to enhance the likelihood that young black males will graduate from high school possessing the skills and motivation to pursue postsecondary vocational training or academic education.

Since the mid-1980s an increasing number of black educators and social scientists have come out in support of alternative educational settings specifically designed to address the academic and developmental needs of young black males at risk of dropping out of school and becoming involved in lifestyles that lead to drug abuse, violence, and other social problems.[5]

The primary rationale for recommending separate classrooms or schools for black males is that traditional educational approaches have failed to retain and graduate a significant number of them into the legitimate opportunity structure. Empirical support for this assertion has been reported in several studies that have found that black males are disproportionately represented among students who drop out of school and those assigned to special education classes, suspended, or expelled. A recent study of the New Orleans public schools, for example, found that black males, who represent 43 percent of the student population, accounted for 80 percent of expulsions and 65 percent of suspensions.[6]

Moreover, advocates of the black male classroom or school have suggested that black males are disadvantaged in attaining an education as a result of their exposure to middle-class white teachers who tend to fear them and are therefore unwilling to nurture their academic and social development.

Thus, advocates of alternative schools or classrooms have recommended that young black males need the opportunity to receive their education in settings in which they are nurtured, exposed to a curriculum that is relevant to their historical experience and cultural heritage, and exposed to black male teachers and other positive male role models.

I support the establishment of separate schools or classrooms for black males who are at risk of becoming involved in assuming masculinity role orientations and lifestyles associated with interpersonal violence. Moreover, these educational environments would be ideal for the implementation of school-based violence-prevention programs that help at-risk adolescents learn and develop conflict resolution skills.[7]

Although separate schools or classrooms for at-risk black males are controversial and have yet to be evaluated, I believe that these educational alternatives represent an innovative violence-prevention strategy that may prove effective in helping young black males achieve role orientations and lifestyles that extend beyond the limited, and often problematic, boundaries of "the streets."

Mentoring and Manhood Development Programs

Mentoring manhood development programs should be established and/or expanded to provide support, structure, and guidance for black males at risk of becoming involved in violent confrontations.

Advocates of separate classrooms or schools for young black males have emphasized the need for positive role models in the lower-class black community as a result of social disorganization from chronic rates of teenage pregnancy, female-headed families, poverty, unemployment, crime, and imprisonment. Consequently, mentoring and manhood development programs are gaining favor among many black academicians and civic and religious leaders as the most viable strategy to prevent violence and other social problems among black males.[8]

Among the programs that currently exist, there is a lack of uniformity in the age range of the target population, curriculum format, and frequency of meetings. However, what is common among these programs is the emphasis they place on transforming young black males into well-functioning men.[9]

The findings of this study have also led me to conclude that community-based institutions and violence-prevention coalitions must create mentoring and manhood development programs not only for young but also for adult black males who are at risk. Representatives of community-based coalitions should encourage masonic lodges, fraternities, and black professional organizations to prevent violence and to become involved in mentoring problematic adult black males.

Finally, coalitions to prevent violence should lobby and pressure politicians and state criminal justice officials to require that violent offenders participate in community-based mentoring and manhood development programs as a condition of probation or parole.

Regardless of the characteristics of the target population, it is important that these programs include age-specific sessions that focus on defining manhood and identity consistent with mainstream expectations, the development of conflict-resolution skills, and strategies to enhance vocational skills and marketability. Ultimately, the primary goal of mentoring and manhood development programs should be to undermine the process by which at-risk lower-class black males define themselves as men by assuming roles and engaging in activities that are valued in "the streets." Mentoring and manhood development programs represent an attempt to provide such black males with viable strategies to avoid role orientations and lifestyles that increase the likelihood of violence participation.

Multicomponent Community Centers

Multicomponent community centers should be established and encouraged to provide programs specifically designed to undermine lower-class black males' attraction to compulsive activities associated with "the streets." Recreational programs should be used as an inducement to encourage young black males to participate in multicomponent community center programs that involve tutoring, counseling, conflict-resolution, and mentoring and manhood development. The Challenger Boys Club, located in Los Angeles, is an example of a model multicomponent community center that has received some national attention for the way it has coordinated its programs to prevent violence and other problematic behavior among black youth.[10]

Multicomponent community centers are an important feature of community-based strategy that I am recommending to reform the social context in which violence among black males occur. The function of these centers is to provide the institutional setting in which blacks develop and institutionalize efforts to prevent violence among black males.

Community Policing

Community policing should be linked to community-based efforts to prevent violence in the black community. Collaborative problem-solving involving the police and local citizens' groups distinguishes community policing from traditional approaches to doing police work. The primary goal of community policing is to prevent crime by solving problems that contribute to it.[11]

Community policing should be implemented in a coordinated fashion with the prevention strategies that I recommended earlier. Organizing high-risk black communities along these lines should facilitate collaborative problem-solving among local community leaders and law-enforcement officials.

Community policing, which emphasizes conspicuous foot patrols and getting to know the members of the community, might prove effective in reducing the occurrence of activities and interactions that lead to violent confrontations in bars and bar settings. I am specifically recommending that community policing details focus attention on patrolling and being present in those settings where low-income black males hang out.

Finally, the specific advantages that can be derived from community policing regarding the prevention of violence among black males involve collaborative efforts to prevent violence and related social problems, and the conspicuous presence of the police in high-risk settings.

Conclusion

At this time, no one is really certain as to what specific policies or programs will substantially reduce the high rates of violence among black males. Findings presented in this study strongly suggest that interactions leading to violent incidents among black males are influenced by role orientations and lifestyles associated with ghetto-based definitions of manhood. Therefore, violence-prevention strategies directed toward reducing violence participation among black males must attempt to change the social context in which young black males enter into manhood.

Appendix:
Barroom Violence Interview Schedule

Type I Incident—Violent Confrontation

Opening Statement

The purpose of this interview is to seek your assistance in helping me to understand the various factors that cause arguments and fights among black males while in bars or bar settings.

This interview is confidential, and I agree not to reveal your name or anything you tell me to anyone who is not directly involved in this research project.

Do you have any questions before we begin?

I. **Description of an Incident that Resulted in a Violent Confrontation in a Bar or Bar Setting**

1. Would you describe the last fight you had with another man in a bar or bar setting (e.g., after-hours joint, greasy spoon restaurant, poolroom, gambling parlor, street corner)?
   Possible Probes:
   When did this occur?
   What happened?
   What started it?

2. Before the fighting started, were you trying to say or tell _____ anything?

165

Possible Probe:
What point were you trying to make?

3. Before the fighting started, what was _____ trying to say or tell you?
   Possible Probe:
   What point was _____ trying to make?

4. Was the argument and fight between you and _____ the result of something that happened between you and while you and he were at the bar or something that happened between you and _____ at some other place?

5. Was the fight between you and _____ about something that one of you had done to someone else?
   Possible Probe:
   Who was the other person (relative, friend, or stranger)?

6. Had you and _____ argued or fought at some other place before you and he argued and fought in the bar?
   Possible Probes:
   Where?
   What happened?

II. Description of How Respondent Accounts for Using Violence to Resolve Interpersonal Conflict

1. What was it about this situation that made it necessary for you to use violence against _____ ?

2. Was there a specific point when you realized that you were going to have to resort to violence in this situation?
   Possible Probe:
   How did you know?

3. What were you trying to accomplish when you hit ?

4. At the time all of this was "going down," how did you feel about how you were handling the situation?

5. Looking back, do you think you handled the situation in the right way?

III. Respondent's Description of the Contribution of Third Parties

1. Were there any other people who got involved in the situation between you and _____ ?
   Possible Probes:
   Who were the other people?
   What were the other people saying/doing?

2. Did anyone encourage you to argue or fight with ?
   Possible Probes:
   Who?
   What did he/they say?

3. Did anyone encourage you not to argue or fight with _____ ?
   Possible Probes:
   Who?
   What did he/they say?

4. Did anyone encourage _____ not to argue or fight with you?
   Possible Probes:
   Who?
   What did he/they say?

5. Did anyone encourage _____ to argue or fight with you?
   Possible Probes:
   Who?
   What did he/they say?

6. How did you feel about what these other people were doing?
   Possible Probes:
   Were you glad?
   Were you afraid?

7. What were the people who were not directly involved in the situation between you and _____ doing?

8. Were you concerned about what the people who were not directly involved were thinking in terms of how you were handling the situation with _____ ?
   Possible Probes:
   What were you concerned about?
   Why weren't you concerned?

9. When all of this was "going down," do you think _____ was concerned about what other people thought about how he was handling the situation with you?
   Possible Probe:
   How do you know he was concerned about what other people thought about the situation?

IV. Respondent's Description of Third-Party Intervention by the Police

1. Are you aware if anyone called the police?
   Possible Probe:
   What did the police say/do?

V. Respondent's Description of How Alcohol and/or Drugs Contributed to the Situation

1. Had you been drinking or "doing drugs" before the fight with _____ ?

2. Do you think alcohol/drugs influenced how you handled the situation with _____ ?

Possible Probes:

How?

Why not?

3. Do you know if _____ had been drinking or "doing drugs" before he and you started fighting?

    Possible Probes:

    How do you know?

    Do you think _____ 's use of alcohol/drugs influenced the way he handled the situation between you and him?

VI. Respondent's Description of Lifestyle Changes Resulting from Participating in a Violent Confrontation in a Bar or Bar Setting

1. After the fight with _____ did you change anything about where you hang out or who you associate with?

    Possible Probe:

    Did you continue going to the bar as often as you had before the fight with _____ ?

2. After the fight with _____ , did you do anything extra to protect yourself?

    Possible Probes:

    Why was it necessary to do that?

    Why wasn't it necessary to do anything extra?

3. What sort of relationship did you and _____ have after the fight?

4. Other than _____ , did anyone start treating you differently because of the fight you had with _____ ?

5. What were people in the street saying about the fight between you and _____ ?

    Possible Probe:

    How did you feel about what was being said in the street?

VII. Respondent's Description of Factors that Cause Violent Confrontations in Bars and Bar settings

1. What causes most fights between guys hanging out in bars and/or the street corners?

2. What are the basic differences between arguments that result in violence and those that do not?

3. How can fights in bars and on the streets be reduced?

VIII. Incident-Related Sociodemographic Data

1. How old were you when this incident occurred?

2. How old was _____ when this incident occurred?

3. What grade were you in at this time?

4. What grade was _____ in at this time?

5. Were you working at the time?

6. Was _____ working at this time?
7. What would be the best estimate of your income at the time this incident occurred?
   Less than $100 per week
   $100 to $150 per week
   $150 to $200 per week
   $200 to $250 per week
   $250 to $300 per week
   $300 to $350 per week
   $350 to $400 per week
   $400 to $450 per week
   $450 to $500 per week
   $500 or more per week
8. Were you married or living with a woman when this incident occurred?
9. Prior to this incident, had you ever been arrested or convicted of any crime?

Type II Incident—Potentially Violent Argument

Opening Statement

The purpose of this interview is to seek your assistance in helping me to understand the various factors that cause arguments and fights among black males while in bars or bar settings.

This interview is confidential and I agree not to reveal your name or anything you tell me to anyone who is not directly involved in this research project.

Do you have any questions before we begin?

I. **Description of an Incident Perceived as Potentially Violent But That Did Not Result in a Violent Confrontation**
   1. Would you describe the last time you had an argument in a bar or bar setting (e.g., after-hours joint, greasy spoon restaurant, pool-room, gambling parlor, street corner) with another man in which you thought that he and you might get into a fight but did not?
      Possible Probes:
      When did this occur?
      What happened?
      What started it?
   2. During the argument, what were you trying to say or tell _____ anything?
      Possible Probe:
      What point were you trying to make?

3. During the argument, what was _____ trying to say or tell you?
   Possible Probe:
   What point was _____ trying to make?
4. Was the argument between you and _____ the result of something that happened between you and _____ while you and he were at the bar or something that happened between you and _____ at some other place?
5. Was the argument between you and _____ about something that one of you had done to someone else?
   Possible Probe:
   Who was the other person (relative, friend, or stranger)?
6. Had you and _____ argued or fought at some other place before you and he argued in the bar?
   Possible Probes:
   Where?
   What happened?

II. Description of How Respondent Accounts for Not Using Violence to Resolve Interpersonal Conflict

1. What was it about this situation that made it unnecessary for you to use violence against _____ ?
2. Was there a specific point when you realized that you were not going to have to resort to violence in this situation?
   Possible Probe:
   How did you know?
3. At the time all of this was "going down," how did you feel about how you were handling the situation?
4. Looking back, do you think you handled the situation in the right way?

III. Respondent's Description of the Contribution of Third Parties

1. Were there any other people who got involved in the situation between you and _____ ?
   Possible Probes:
   Who were the other people?
   What were the other people saying/doing?
2. Did anyone encourage you to argue or fight with _____ ?
   Possible Probes:
   Who?
   What did he/they say?
3. Did anyone encourage you not to argue or fight with _____ ?
   Possible Probes:
   Who?
   What did he/they say?

4. Did anyone encourage _____ not to argue or fight with you?
   Possible Probes:
   Who?
   What did he/they say?
5. Did anyone encourage _____ to argue or fight with you?
   Possible Probes:
   Who?
   What did he/they say?
6. How did you feel about what these other people were doing?
   Possible Probes:
   Were you glad?
   Were you afraid?
7. What were the people who were not directly involved in the situation between you and _____ doing?
8. Were you concerned about what the people who were not directly involved were thinking in terms of how you were handling the situation with _____ ?
   Possible Probes:
   What were you concerned about?
   Why weren't you concerned?
9. When all of this was "going down," do you think _____ was concerned about what other people thought about how he was handling the situation with you?
   Possible Probe:
   How do you know he was concerned about what other people thought about the situation?

IV. Respondent's Description of Third-Party Intervention by the Police

1. Are you aware if anyone called the police?
   Possible Probe:
   What did the police say/do?

V. Respondent's Description of How Alcohol and/or Drugs Contributed to the Situation

1. Had you been drinking or "doing drugs" before the argument with
   _____ ?
2. Do you think alcohol/drugs influenced how you handled the situation with _____ ?
   Possible Probes:
   How?
   Why not?

3. Do you know if _____ had been drinking or "doing drugs" before he and you started fighting?
   Possible Probes:
   How do you know?
   Do you think _____ 's use of alcohol/drugs influenced the way he handled the situation between you and he? How?

VI. Respondent's Description of Lifestyle Changes Resulting from Participating in a Potentially Violent Argument in a Bar or Bar Setting

1. After the argument with _____ did you change anything about where you hang out or who you associate with?
   Possible Probe:
   Did you continue going to the bar as often as you had before the argument with _____ ?

2. After the argument with _____ , did you do anything extra to protect yourself?
   Possible Probes:
   Why was it necessary to do that?
   Why wasn't it necessary to do anything extra?

3. What sort of relationship did you and _____ have after the argument?

4. Other than _____ , did anyone start treating you differently because of the argument you had with _____ ?

5. What were people in the street saying about the argument between you and _____ ?
   Possible Probe:
   How did you feel about what was being said in the street?

VII. Respondent's Description of Factors that Cause Argument and Violent Confrontation in Bars and Bar Settings

1. What causes most of the arguments between guys hanging out in the bars and/or the street corners?
2. What are the basic differences between arguments that result in violence and those that do not?
3. How can fights in bars and on the streets be reduced?

VIII. Incident-Related Sociodemographic Data

1. How old were you when this incident occurred?
2. How old was _____ when this incident occurred?
3. What grade were you in at this time?
4. What grade was _____ in at this time?
5. Were you working at the time?
6. Was _____ working at this time?

7. What would be the best estimate of your income at the time this incident occurred?

   Less than $100 per week
   $100 to $150 per week
   $150 to $200 per week
   $200 to $250 per week
   $250 to $300 per week
   $300 to $350 per week
   $350 to $400 per week
   $400 to $450 per week
   $450 to $500 per week
   $500 or more per week

8. Were you married or living with a woman when this incident occurred?

9. Prior to this incident, had you ever been arrested or convicted of any crime?

Notes

Chapter 1: Violence Among Black Males

1. Sessions, 1990.
2. For a full review of violent crime data sources and local studies of criminal homicide, see Bureau of Justice Statistics, 1990; Centers for Disease Control, 1985, 1990; Curtis, 1974; Harper, 1976; Voss and Hepburn, 1968; and Wilbanks, 1984.
3. Centers for Disease Control, 1990; U.S. Department of Health, 1992, p. 76.
4. Bureau of Justice Statistics, 1990.
5. Hannerz, 1969, p. 65.
6. Sargent, 1986, p. C4.
7. Schultz, 1960.
8. Sterne and Pittman, 1972; Samuels, 1976.
9. Toch, 1980b, p. 647.
10. Curtis, 1975; Bureau of Justice Statistics, 1990.
11. Blumer, 1980, p. xi.
12. Cohen and Felson, 1979, p. 593.

Chapter 2: Perspectives on Causation

1. For a full review of theoretical perspectives on the causes of violence among blacks, see Bell, 1987; Curtis, 1975; Dollard, 1937; Gary, 1983, 1986; Harper, 1976; Hawkins, 1983; Williams, 1984; and Wolfgang and Ferracuti, 1967.
2. Frazier, 1949; Shaw and McKay, 1942.

3. Wolfgang, 1983.
4. Bailey 1984; Blau and Blau, 1982; Williams, 1984.
5. Banfield, 1970; Miler, 1958.
6. Cloward and Ohlen, 1960; Cohen, 1955; Merton, 1938, 1957.
7. Davis, 1976; *Ebony*, 1979; G. Johnson, 1941; Silberman, 1978; and Staples, 1974, 1975, 1982, 1984.
8. Dollard, 1937, p. 252. See also Grier and Cobb, 1968; Pettigrew, 1964; and Powdermaker, 1943.
9. Blauner, 1972; Higginbotham, 1978; Knowles and Prewitt, 1969.
10. Pettigrew, 1964, pp. 151–52. See also Poussaint, 1972.
11. Wolfgang and Ferracuti, 1967.
12. Miller, 1958.
13. Curtis, 1975, p. 18.
14. Hannerz, 1969, pp. 65, 87–89; Curtis, 1975, pp. 23–35, 49–54.
15. Clark, 1965; Cloward and Ohlin, 1960; Toby, 1966; Staples, 1982; and Oliver, 1984, 1989a.
16. Parsons, 1947.
17. For a full discussion of literature that examines compulsive masculinity see Hannerz, 1969; Liebow, 1967; Matza, 1964; Milner and Miller, 1972; Rainwater, 1970; and Vontress, 1971.
18. Toby, 1966.
19. Banfield, 1970; Frazier, 1949; Miller, 1958; and Moynihan, 1965.
20. Miller, 1958.
21. Hannerz, 1969, p. 112. See also Rainwater, 1970, p. 393.
22. Staples, 1982; Oliver, 1984, 1989a.
23. U.S. Bureau of Census, 1983.
24. Frazier, 1949; Miller, 1958; Moynihan, 1965.
25. Dollard, 1937, p. 280.
26. Wolfgang, 1958, pp. 188–89.
27. Erlanger, 1974; Ball-Roheach, 1973.
28. Brownfield, 1987.
29. Wolfgang, 1958.
30. Goodman et al., 1986.
31. Pittman and Handy, 1964.
32. Zahn and Snodgrass, 1978.
33. Zahn and Bencivengo, 1974.
34. Tardiff et al., 1986.
35. Bureau of Justice Statistics, 1988.

Chapter 3: Black Bars: Social Functions and Compulsive Masculinity Displays

1. *American Heritage Dictionary*, 1979.
2. Clinard, 1962, 279.

3. Macrory, 1952.
4. Cavan, 1966, p. 265.
5. Samuels, 1976, pp. 51, 97.
6. Lewis, 1955, p. 66; Samuels, 1976, pp. 41, 51–57; and Sterne and Pittman, 1972, pp. 248–253.
7. Lewis, 1955; Samuels, 1976.
8. Goffman, 1957, pp. 241–242.
9. Lyman and Scott, 1970b, p. 145.
10. Folb, 1980, p. 127.
11. Rainwater, 1970, p. 206.
12. Goffman, 1957, p. 22.
13. Majors and Mancini Billson, 1992.
14. Cooke, 1972.
15. Suttles, 1968; Cooke, 1972.
16. Dollard, 1939; Abrahams, 1970.
17. Suttles, 1968; Hannertz, 1969; Samuels, 1976; Anderson, 1976.
18. For a discussion of woofing, see Cooke, 1972, p. 44; Folb, 1980, pp. 103–108; and Kochman, 1981, p. 49.
19. Schwartz, 1963.
20. Folb, 1980, p. 111.
21. Hannerz, 1969, p. 80.
22. Cooke, 1972, pp. 52–54.
23. Hannerz, 1969, p. 887.
24. Samuels, 1976, p. 52.
25. Kochman, 1981, p. 16.
26. For a full discussion of the interpersonal dynamics of male-female rapping, see Kochman, 1981, and Samuels, 1976.
27. Hannerz, 1969, p. 85.
28. Hannerz, 1969, p. 85.
29. Blassingame, 1972.
30. Miller, 1958.

Chapter 4: Toward the Development of a Conceptual Framework

1. Graham et al., 1980.
2. Campbell and Marsh, 1979.
3. Graham and Trumbull, 1978.
4. Felson and Steadman, 1983, p. 163.
5. Marsh, 1980, p. 211.
6. Felson, et al., 1986.
7. Felson, et al., 1986, p. 157.
8. Marsh, 1980.
9. See Anderson, 1976; Hannerz, 1969; Liebow, 1967; Rainwater, 1970; and Samuels, 1976.
10. Oliver, 1989a.

11. Hindelang, et al., 1978; and Cohen and Felson, 1979.
12. Hindelang, et al., 1978, p. 242.
13. Hindelang, et al., 1978, p. 242.
14. Cohen and Felson, 1979, p. 589.
15. Cohen and Felson, 1979, p. 589.
16. Center on Budget and Policy Priorities, 1986.
17. Wilson and Neckerman, 1987.
18. Blumer, 1969.
19. Athens, 1980, p. 16; 1986, p. 376.
20. Stokes and Hewitt, 1976, p. 843.

Chapter 5: Methods and Sample

1. For a full discussion of the phenomenological approach, see Allport, 1942; Bogan and Taylor, 1975; Brown and Sime, 1981; and Martin, et al., 1968.
2. Toch, 1969.
3. Polsky, 1967; Milner and Milner, 1972; and Klockars, 1974.
4. Toch, 1975.
5. Lockwood, 1980.
6. Johnson, 1981.
7. Dobash and Dobash, 1984.
8. Scully, 1990; Scully and Marolla, 1984.
9. Merton and Kendall, 1946.
10. Anderson, 1976, p. 1.
11. Prior to interviewing respondents, I gathered preliminary information about violence in local bars and bar settings from informed local residents, police officers and representatives of the county prosecutor's office.
12. Toch, 1969; Athens, 1980; Levir, 1980; Felson, 1982; and Ray and Simons, 1987.
13. Toch, 1969, p. 5.
14. Brown and Sime, 1981, p. 166.
15. Paul, 1965; Newson and Newson, 1972.
16. Brown and Sime, 1981, p. 167.
17. Lyman and Scott, 1970a, p. 112.
18. Brown and Sime, 1981, p. 160.
19. Acker, 1977; Goode, 1978.
20. Meier, 1981, p. 12.
21. Toch, 1969, p. 195.
22. Miller, 1958; Clark, 1965; Liebow, 1967; Hannerz, 1969; Staples, 1974.
23. I have deliberately deleted the reference to the census data to conceal the location of the research site.

Chapter 6: Hanging Out

1. Goffman, 1967a, p. 171.
2. Goffman, 1967b, p. 49.

Chapter 7: The Violence Process

1. Hepburn, 1973; Luckenbill, 1977.
2. Lyman and Scott, 1970a, p. 112.
3. Stokes and Hewitt, 1976, p. 843.
4. Toch, 1986, p. 33.
5. Luckenbill, 1977.

Chapter 8: Discussion of Findings

1. Toch, 1969, p. 135.
2. Toch, 1969, p. 135.
3. Toch, 1969, p. 135.
4. Hannerz, 1969, p. 82.
5. Horowitz, 1985, p. 23.
6. See Gouldner, 1960; Mauss, 1954; Palmer, 1972.
7. Palmer, 1972, p. 59.
8. Hewitt, 1976, p. 109.
9. Stokes and Hewitt, 1976, p. 843.
10. Sykes and Matza, 1957.
11. Black, 1983.
12. Sykes and Matza, 1987, p. 668.
13. Hepburn, 1973.
14. Hepburn, 1973.
15. Felson and Steadman, 1983.
16. Luckenbill, 1987; Levi, 1980.
17. Athens, 1985, p. 431.
18. Berkowitz, 1978; Katz, 1988.
19. Duncan, 1968.
20. Katz, 1988.
21. Katz, 1988, p. 24.
22. Felson, et al., 1986; Graham and Trumbull, 1978.

Chapter 9: Research and Prevention Implications

1. Prothrow-Stith, 1991; Secretary's Task Force on Black and Minority Health, 1986.
2. Eisenhower Foundation, 1990.
3. Currie, 1986; Curtis, 1985; Eisenhower Foundation, 1990; Wilson, 1990.
4. Newman, 1979.
5. See Kunjufu, 1982, 1986, 1991; and Holland, 1987, 1989.
6. Tift, 1990.
7. Prothrow-Stith, 1987, 1991.
8. Oliver, 1989a; Wilson-Brewer and Jacklin, 1990.
9. Hill, 1992.
10. Wilson-Brewer and Jacklin, 1990.
11. L. Brown, 1990.

References

Abrahams, R. D.(1964). *Deep Down in the Jungle.* Hatboro, PA: Folklore Associates.
——— (1970). *Positively Black.* Englewood Cliffs, NJ: Prentice-Hall.
——— (1972). "Joking: The Training of the Man of Words in Talking Broad," in T. Kochman (ed.), *Rappin' and Stylin' Out.* Chicago: University of Illinois Press, pp. 215–40.
Acker, R. L. (1977). *Deviant Behavior: A Social Learning Perspective.* Belmont CA: Wadsworth.
Allen, J. (1978). *Assault with a Deadly Weapon: The Autiobiography of a Street Criminal.* New York: Pantheon Books
Allport, G. W. (1942). *The Use of Personal Documents in Psychological Science.* New York: Social Science Research Council.
American Heritage Dictionary (1979). Boston: Houghton Mifflin Company.
Anderson, E. (1976). *A Place on the Corner.* Chicago: University of Chicago Press.
Athens, L. H. (1980). *Violent Criminal Acts and Actors.* Boston: Routledge and Kegan Paul.
——— (1985). "Character Contests and Violent Criminal Conduct: A Critique." *Sociology Quarterly* 26:419–31.
Bailey, W. C. (1984). "Poverty, Inequality, and City Homicide Rates. Some Not Expected Findings." *Criminology* 22:531–56.
Baldwin, J. A., and Y. R. Bell (1985). "The African Self-Consciousness Scale: An Afrocentric Personality Questionnaire." *Western Journal of Black Studies* 9:61–68.
Banfield, E. C. (1970). *The Unheavenly City: The Nature and Future of Our Urban Crisis.* Boston: Little, Brown and Company.
Bell, C. (1987). "Prevention Strategies for Dealing with Violence Among Blacks." *Community Mental Health Journal* 23:217–28.

Bensing, R. C., and O. Schroder (1960). *Homicide in an Urban Community.* Springfield, IL: Charles C. Thomas.

Berkowitz, L. (1978). "Is Criminal Violence Normative Behavior?: Hostile and Instrumental Aggression in Violent Incidents." *Journal of Research in Crime and Delinquency* 15:148–61.

Billingsley, A. (1968). *Black Families in White America.* Englewood Cliffs, NJ: Prentice-Hall.

Black, D. (1983). "Crime as Social Control." *American Sociological Review* 48:34–45.

Blassingame, J. (1972). *The Slave Community.* New York: Oxford University Press.

Blau, J. R., and P. M. Blau (1982). "The Cost of Inequality: Metropolitan Structure and Violent Crime." *American Sociological Review* 47:114–29.

Blauner, R. (1972). *Racial Oppression in America.* New York: Harper and Row.

Blumer, H. (1962). "Society as Symbolic Interaction," in A. Rose (ed.), *Human Behavior and Social Processes.* Boston: Houghton Mifflin, pp. 179–92.

——— (1969). *Symbolic Interactionism: Perspective and Method.* Englewood Cliffs, NJ: Prentice-Hall.

——— (1980). "Foreword," in L. H. Athens, *Violent Criminal Acts and Actors—A Symbolic Interactionists Study.* Boston: Routledge and Kegan Paul, pp. ix–xii.

Bogan, R., and S. J. Taylor (1975). *Introduction to Qualitative Research Methods.* New York: John Wiley.

Bonger, W. A. (1943). *Race and Crime.* New York: Columbia University Press.

Borden, R. J. "Witnessed Aggression: Influence of an Observer's Sex and Values on Aggressive Responding." *Journal of Personality and Social Psychology* 3:354–61.

Boudouris, J. (1971). "Homicide and the Family". *Journal of Marriage and the Family,* 33:667–76.

Bourne, R. G. (1973). "Alcoholism in the Urban Negro Population," in P. G. Bourne and R. Fox (eds.), *Alcoholism Progress in Research and Treatment.* New York: Academic Press, pp. 211–25.

Braithwaite, R. L. (1981). "Interpersonal Relations Between Black Males and Females," in L. Gary (ed.), *Black Men.* Beverly Hills: Sage Publications, pp. 83–97.

Brearly, H. C. (1932). *Homicide in the United States.* Chapel Hill, NC: University of North Carolina Press.

Brenton, M. (1966). *The American Male.* New York: Coward-McCann.

Brown, J., and J. Sime (1981). "A methodology for accounts," in M. Brenner (ed.), *Social Method and Social Life.* New York: Academic Press, pp. 159–88.

Brown, L. P. (1990). "Community Policing: A Practical Guide for Police Officials." In U.S. Department of Justice, *Perspectives on Policing.* Washington, DC: Government Printing Office, pp. 1–11.

Brownfield, D. (1987). "Father-Son Relationships and Violent Behavior." *Deviant Behavior* 8:65–78.

Bureau of Justice Statistics (1990). *Criminal Victimization in the United States, 1990.* Washington, DC: U. S. Department of Justice.

——— (1988). Drug Use and Crime. Washington, DC: U.S. Department of Justice.

Campbell, A. (1986). "The Streets and Violence," in A. Campbell and J. Gibbs (eds.), *Violent Transactions.* New York: Basil Blackwell.

Campbell, A., and J. Gibbs (eds.) (1986). *Violent Transactions.* New York: Basil Blackwell.

Campbell, A. and P. Marsh (1979). Final Report to Whitbread Ltd., Oxford: Contemporary Violence Research Centre, Oxford University.

Cavan, S. (1966). *Liquor License: An Ethnography of Bar Behavior.* Chicago: Aldine.

Cazanave, N. A. (1981). "Black Men in America: The Quest for Manhood," in L. Gray (ed.), *Black Men.* Beverly Hills: Sage Publications pp. 176–85.

Centers for Disease Control (1985). "Homicide Among Young Black Males—United States, 1970–1982." *Morbidity and Mortality Weekly Report* 34 (41):629–33.

——— (1990). "Homicide Among Young Black Males—United States, 1978–1987." *Morbidity and Mortality Weekly Report* 39 (48):869–73.

Center on "Budget and Policy Priorities (1986). Falling Behind—A Report on How Blacks Have Fared Under Reagan." *Journal of Black Studies* 17:148–172.

Clark, K. B. (1965). *Dark Ghetto: Dilemmas of Social Power.* New York: Harper and Row.

Clinard, M. B. (1962). "The Public Drinking House and Society," in D. J. Pittman and C. R. Snyder (eds.), *Society, Culture, and Drinking Patterns.* New York: John Wiley, pp. 270–92.

Cloward, R. A., and L. E. Ohlin (1960). *Delinquency and Opportunity.* New York: Free Press.

Cohen, A. (1955). *Delinquent Boys.* New York: Free Press.

Cohen, L. E., and M. Felson (1979). "Social Change and Crime Trends: A Routine Activity Approach." *American Sociological Review* 44:588–608.

Cooke. B. G. (1972). "Nonverbal Communication Among Afro-Americans: An Initial Classification," in T. Kochman (ed.), *Rappin' and Stylin' Out: Communication in Urban Black America.* Chicago: University of Illinois Press, pp. 32–64.

Cromwell, W. O. (1948). *The Tavern in Relation to Children and Youth.* Chicago: Chicago Juvenile Protective Association.

Currie, E. (1986). "Crimes of Violence and Public Policy: Changing Directions," in L. A. Curtis (ed.), *American Violence and Public Policy.* New Haven, CT: Yale University Press, pp. 41–62.

Curtis, L. A. (1974). *Criminal Violence.* Lexington, MA: Lexington Books.

——— (1975). *Violence, Race and Culture.* Lexington, MA: Lexington Books.

——— (1985). "Neighborhood, Family, and Employment: Toward a New Public Policy Against Violence," in L. A. Curtis (ed.), *American Violence and Public Policy.* New Haven, CT: Yale University Press, pp. 205–24.

Davis, J. A. (1976). "Blacks, Crime and American Culture." *Annals of the American Academy of Political and Social Science* 423:89–98.

Dennis, R. E. (1977). "Social Stress and Mortality Among Nonwhite Males." *Phylon* 38:213–28.

——— (1979). "The Role of Homicide in Decreasing Life Expectancy," in H. M. Rose (ed.), *Lethal Aspects of Urban Violence.* Lexington, MA: Lexington Books.

Denzin, N. K. (1984). "Toward a Phenomenology of Domestic Family Violence." *American Journal of Sociology* 90:483–513.

Dinitz, S. (1951). "The Relation of the Tavern to the Drinking Phases of Alcoholics." Ph.D. Diss. Madison: University of Wisconsin.

Dobash, R. E., and R. T. Dobash (1984). "The Nature and Antecedents of Violent Events." *British Journal of Criminology* (24):269–88.

Dollard, J. (1937). *Caste and Caste in a Southern Town.* Garden City, NY: Doubleday Anchor Books.

Dollard, J., et al. (1939). *Frustration and Aggression*. New Haven, CT: Yale University Press.

Duncan, H. D. (1969). *Symbols in Society*. New York: Oxford University Press.

Ebony (1979). "Black-on-Black Crime." Vol. 34 (August):6–146.

Eisenhower Foundation (1990). *Youth Investment and Community Reconstruction— Street Lessons on Drugs and Crime for the Nineties*. Washington, DC: Milton Eisenhower Foundation.

Erlanger, H. S. (1974). "The Empirical Status of the Subculture of Violence Thesis." *Social Problems* 22:280–291.

Felson, R. B. (1978). "Aggression as Impression Management." *Social Psychology* 41:205–13.

——— (1982). "Impression Management and the Escalation of Aggression and Violence." *Social Psychology Quarterly* 45:245–54.

Felson, R. B., and H. S. Steadman (1983). "Situations and Processes Leading to Criminal Violence." *Criminology* 21:59–74.

Felson, R. B., S. A. Ribner, and M. S. Siegel (1984). "Age and the Effect of the Third Parties During Criminal Violence." *Sociology and Social Research* 68(4):452–62.

Felson, R. B., et al. (1986). "Barroom Brawls: Aggression and Violence in Irish and American Bars," in A. Campbell and J. J. Gibbs (eds.), *Violent Transactions—The Limits of Personality*. New York: Basil Blackwell, pp. 153–66.

Felson, R. B., and J. T. Tedeschi (1991). "A Theory of Coercive Actions: An Integration of Research on Conflict, Influence, Aggression, and Violent Crime." Unpublished manuscript.

Folb, E. A. (1980). *Runnin' Down Some Lines: The Language and Culture of Black Teenagers*. Cambridge, MA: Harvard University Press.

Frazier, E. F. (1949). *The Negro Family in the United States*. Chicago: University of Chicago Press.

Gary, L. (1983). "The Impact of Alcohol and Drug Abuse on Homicidal Violence," in T. D. Watts and R. Wright (eds.), *Black Alcoholism—Toward a Comprehensive Understanding*. Springfield, IL: Charles C. Thomas, pp. 136–51.

——— (1986). "Drinking, Homicide and the Black Male." *Journal of Black Studies* 17:15–31.

Gastil, R. D. (1971). "Homicide and the Regional Culture of Violence." *American Sociological Review* 36:412–26.

Gibbs, J. J. (1986). "Alcohol Consumption, Cognition and Violence," in A. Campbell and J. J. Gibbs (eds.), *Violent Transactions*. New York: Basil Blackwell.

Glasgow, D. G. (1980). *The Black Underclass: Poverty, Unemployment and Entrapment of Ghetto Youth*. New York: Vintage Books.

Goetting, A. (1988). "Patterns of Homicide Among Women." *Journal of Interpersonal Violence* 3:3–20.

Goffman, E. (1957). *The Presentation of Self in Everyday Life*. Garden City, NY: Doubleday Anchor Books.

Goffman, E. (1967a). "Where the Action Is," in E. Goffman (ed.), Interaction Ritual: Essays on Face-to-Face Behavior. Garden City, NY: Anchor Books, pp. 149–270.

——— (1967b). "The Nature of Deference and Demeanor," in E. Goffman (ed.), *Interaction Ritual: Essays on Face-to-Face Behavior*. Garden City, NY: Anchor Books, pp. 47–95.

Goldstein, P. J. (1985). "The Drugs/Violence Nexus: A Tripartite Conceptual Framework." Journal of Drug Issues 14:493–506.

Goffman, E. (1967a). "Where the Action Is" in E. Goffman (ed.), *Interaction Ritual*. Garden City, N.Y.: Anchor Books.

Goode, W. J. (1978). *The Celebration of Heroes*. Berkeley: University of California Press.

Goodman, R. A., et al. (1986). "Alcohol and Interpersonal Violence: Alcohol Detected in Homicide Victims." *American Journal of Public Health* 76:144–49.

Gottlieb, D. (1957). "The Neighborhood Bar and the Cocktail Lounge: A Study of Class Differences." *American Journal of Sociology* 62:559–62.

Gouldner, A. (1960). "The Norm of Reciprocity." *American Sociological Review* 25:161–71.

Graham, K., et al. (1980). "Aggression and Barroom Environments." *Journal of Studies on Alcohol* 41:277–92.

Graham, K., and W. Trumbull (1978). "Alcohol and Naturally Occurring Aggression." Paper presented at a meeting of the Western Psychological Association, April 1978.

Grier, W. H., and P. M. Cobb (1968). *Black Rage*. New York: Basic Books.

Hannerz, U. (1969). *Soulside: Inquiries into Ghetto Culture*. New York: Columbia University Press.

Hare, N. (1964). "The Frustrated Masculinity of the Negro Male." *Negro Digest*, pp. 5–9.

Harper, F. (1976). "Alcohol and Crime in Black America," in F. Harper (ed.), *Alcohol Abuse and Black America*. Alexandria, VA: Douglas Publisher, pp. 129–40.

Hawkins, D. F. (1983). "Black and White Homicide Differentials—Alternatives to an Adequate Theory." *Criminal Justice and Behavior* 10:407–40.

——— (1985). "Black Homicide: The Adequacy of Existing Research for Devising Prevention Strategies." *Crime and Delinquency* 31:83–109.

Hepburn, J. R. (1973). "Violent Behavior in Interpersonal Relationships." *Sociological Quarterly* 14:419–29.

Hewitt, J. P. (1976). *Self and Society—A Symbolic Interactionist Social Psychology*. Boston: Allyn and Bacon.

Higginbotham, L. A. (1978). *In the Matter of Color—The Colonial Period*. New York: Oxford University Press.

Hill, P. (1992). Coming of Age—African American Male Rites-of-Passage. Chicago: African American Images.

Hindelang, M., et al. (1978). *Victims of Personal Crime: An Empirical Foundation for a Theory of Personal Victimization*. Cambridge, MA: Ballinger.

Holland, S. (1987). "A Radical Approach to Educating Young Black Males." *Education Week*, March 25, p. 24.

——— (1989). "Fighting the Epidemic of Failure—A Radical Strategy for Educating Inner-City Boys." *Teacher Magazine*, September/October, pp. 88–89.

Horowitz, R. (1985). *Honor and the American Dream—Culture and Identity in a Chicago Community*. New Brunswick, NJ: Rutgers University Press.

Horowitz, R., and Schwartz, G. (1974). "Honor, Normative Ambiguity and Gang Violence." *American Sociological Review* 39:238–51.

Horton, J. (1972). "Time and Cool People," in T. Kochman (ed.), *Rappin' and Stylin' Out*. Chicago: University of Illinois Press.

Johnson, G. (1941). "The Negro and Crime." *Annals of the American Academy of Political and Social Science* 27:93–104.

Johnson, R. (1981). *Condemned to Die: Life Under Sentence of Death.* New York: Elsevier.

Jones, B. J., et al. (1988). *Social Problems—Issues, Opinions and Solutions.* New York: McGraw-Hill.

Jones, J. M. (1972). *Prejudice and Racism.* Reading, MA: Addison, Wesley.

Katz, J. (1988). *Seductions of Crime—Moral and Sensual Attractions in Doing Evil.* New York: Basic Books.

Klockars, C. B. (1974). *The Professional Fence.* New York: Free Press.

Knowles, L. L., and K. Prewitt (eds.) (1969). *Institutional Racism in America.* Englewood Cliffs, NJ: Prentice-Hall.

Kochman, T. (ed.) (1972). *Rappin' and Stylin' Out.* Chicago: University of Illinois Press.

―――― (1972). "Toward an Ethnography of Black American Speech Behavior," in T. Kochman, *Rappin' and Stylin' Out.* Chicago: University of Illinois Press, pp. 241–64.

―――― (1981). *Black and White Styles in Conflict.* Chicago: University of Chicago Press.

Kunjufu, J. (1982). *Countering the Conspiracy to Destroy Black Boys,* vol. 1. Chicago: African-American Images.

―――― (1986). *Countering the Conspiracy to Destroy Black Boys,* vol. 2. Chicago: African-American Images.

―――― (1991). *Countering the Conspiracy to Destroy Black Boys,* vol. 3. Chicago: African-American Images.

Lawton, M. (1990). "Two Schools Aimed for Black Males Set in Milwaukee." *Education Week,* October 10, p. 1.

LeMasters, E. E. (1975). *Blue-Collar Aristocrats: Lifestyles at a Working-Class Tavern.* Madison: University of Wisconsin.

Levi, K. (1980). "Homicide as Conflict Resolution." *Deviant Behavior* 1:281–307.

Lewis, H. (1955). *Blackways of Kent.* Chapel Hill, NC: University of North Carolina Press.

Liebow, E. (1967). *Tally's Corner.* Boston: Little, Brown, and Company.

Lockwood, D. (1980). *Prison Sexual Violence.* New York: Elsevier.

Lofland, J. (1971). *Analyzing Social Settings: A Grind to Qualitative Observation and Analysis.* Belmont, CA: Wadsworth.

Loftin, C., and R. Hill (1974). "Regional Subculture Homicide: An Examination of the Gastil-Hackney Thesis." *American Sociologist Review* 39:714–24.

Luckenbill, D. F. (1977). "Criminal Homicide as a Situated Transaction." *Social Problems* 25:176–86.

―――― (1987). "Character Contests and Violent Criminal Conduct: A Critique," in N. K. Denzin (ed.), *Studies in Symbolic Interaction.* Greenwich, CT: JAI Press.

Lyman, S. M., and M. B. Scott (1970a). "Accounts," in S. M. Lyman and M. B. Scott (eds.), *Sociology of the Absurd.* New York: Appleton-Century-Crofts, pp. 111–43.

―――― (1970b). "Coolness in Everyday Life," in S. M. Lyman and M. B. Scott (eds.), *A Sociology of the Absurd.* New York: Appleton-Century-Crofts, pp. 145–55.

Macrory, B. E. (1952). "The Tavern and the Community." *Quarterly Journal of Studies on Alcohol* 13:609–37.

Madhubuti, H. R. (1990). *Black Men: Obsolete, Single, and Dangerous?* Chicago: Third World Press.

Majors, R., and J. Mancini Billson (1992). *Cool Pose—The Dilemmas of Black Manhood in America.* New York: Lexington Books.

Marsh, P. (1980). "Violence at the Pub." *New Society* 12:210–12.

Martin. J. M., et al. (1968). *The Analysis of Delinquent Behavior: A Structural Approach.* New York: Random House.

Matza, D. (1964). *Delinquency and Drift.* New York: John Wiley.

Mauss, M. (1954). *The Gift.* Glencoe, IL: Free Press.

Meier, R. F. (1981). "Norms and the Study of Deviance: A Proposed Research Strategy." *Deviant Behavior* 3:1–25.

Meredith, W. (1984). "The Murder Epidemic." *Science* 84:42.

Merton, R. K. (1938). "Social Structure and Anomie." *American Sociological Review* 3:672–82.

——— (1957). *Social Theory and Social Structure.* New York: Free Press.

Merton, R. K., and P. L. Kendall (1946). "The Focused Interview." *American Journal of Sociology* 51:541–57.

Miller, W. (1958). "Lower Class Culture as a Generality Milieu of Gang Delinquency." *Journal of Social Issues* 14:5–19.

Mills, C. W. (1940). "Situated Actions and Vocabularies of Motive," *American Sociological Review* 5:904–13.

Milner, C., and R. Milner (1972). *Black Players: The Secret World of Black Pimps.* Boston: Little, Brown.

Mitchell-Kernan, C. (1972). "Signifying, Loud-Talking, and Marking," in T. Kochman (ed.), *Rappin' and Stylin' Out.* Chicago: University of Illinois Press, pp. 315–35.

Mostyn, B. (1985). "The Content Analysis of Qualitative Research Data: A Dynamic Approach," in M. Brenner et al. (eds.), *The Research Interview.* London: Academic Press.

Moynihan, D. (1965). *The Negro Family: The Case for National Action.* Office of Policy, Planning and Research, Department of Labor. Washington, DC: Government Printing Office.

National Center for Health Statistics (1984). "Advance Report of Final Mortality Statistics, 1982." *Monthly Vital Statistics Report* 33:1–6.

Newman, G. (1979). *Understanding Violence.* Philadelphia: J. B. Lippincott.

Newson, J., and E. Newson (1972). *Seven Year Old in the Home Environment.* London: Routledge and Kegan Paul.

Oliver, W. (1984). "Black Males and the Tough Guy Image: A Dysfunctional Compensatory Adaptation." *Western Journal of Black Studies* 8:199–203.

——— (1989a). "Black Males and Social Problems: Prevention Through Afrocentric Socialization." *Journal of Black Studies* 20:15–39.

——— (1989b). "Sexual Conquest and Patterns of Black-on-Black Violence: A Structural-Cultural Perspective." *Violence and Victims* 4:257–71.

Palmer, S. (1972). *The Violent Society.* New Haven, CT: College and University Press.

Parsons, T. (1947). "Certain Primary Sources of Aggression in the Social Structure of the Western World." *Psychiatry* 10:167–81.

Paul, B. (1965). "Anthropology Today," in A. Kroeber (ed.), *Anthropology Today.* Chicago: University of Chicago Press, pp. 430–51.

Pecar, J. (1972). "Involved Bystanders: Examination of a Neglected Aspect of Criminology and Victimology." *International Journal of Contemporary Sociology* 1:18–42.

Perkins, U. (1975). *Home is a Dirty Street: The Social Oppression of Black Youth.* Chicago: Third World Press.

Pettigrew, T. F. (1964). *A Profile of the Negro American.* Princeton: Van Nostrand.

Pfautz, H. W., and R. W. Hyde (1960). "The Ecology of Alcohol in the Local Community." *Quarterly Journal of Studies on Alcohol* 21:477–66.

Pittman, D. J., and W. Handy (1964). "Patterns in Criminal Aggravated Assault." *Journal of Criminal Law, Criminology and Police Science* 55:462–70.

Pokorny, A. D. (1965). "Human Violence: A Comparison of Homicide, Aggravated Assault, Suicide, and Attempted Suicide." *Journal of Criminal Law, Criminology and Police Science* 56:488–97.

Polsky, N. (1967). *Hustlers, Beats, and Others.* Chicago: Aldine.

Poussaint, A. F. (1972). *Why Blacks Kill Other Blacks.* New York: Emerson Hall.

——— (1983). "Black on-Black Homicide: A Psychological Perspective." *Victimology* 8: 161–69.

Powdermaker, H. (1943). "The Channeling of Negro Aggression by the Cultural Process." *American Journal of Sociology* 48:750–58.

Prothrow-Stith, D. (1987). *Violence Prevention Curriculum for Adolescents.* Newton, MA: Education Development Center.

——— (1991). *Deadly Consequences.* New York: HarperCollins.

Rainwater, L. (1970). *Behind Ghetto Walls: Black Families in a Federal Slum.* Chicago: Aldine.

Ray, M. C., and R. L. Simonson (1987). "Convicted Murderers' Accounts of Their Crimes: A Study of Homicide in Small Communities." *Symbolic Interaction* 10:57–70.

Rose, H. M. (1986). "Can We Substantially Lower Homicide Risk in the Nation's Larger Black Communities," in *Report of the Secretary's Task Force on Black and Minority Health.* Washington, DC: U.S. Department of Health and Human Services, pp. 185–221.

Robins, L. N., G. E. Murphy, and M. B. Breckenridge (1968). "Drinking Behavior of Young Urban Negro Men." *Quarterly Journal of Studies on Alcohol* 29:657–84.

Roebuck, J., and L. S. Spray (1967). "The Cocktail Lounge: A Study of Heterosexual Relations in a Public Organization." *American Journal of Sociology* 72:388–95.

Rosen, L. (1970). "Matriarchy and Lower Class Negro Male Delinquency." *Social Problems* 17:175–89.

Rubin, J. Z. (1980). "Experimental Research on Third Party Intervention in Conflict: Toward Some Generalizations." *Psychological Bulletin* 87:379–91.

Samuels, F. G. (1976). *The Negro Tavern: A Microcosm of Slum Life.* San Francisco: R&E Research Associates.

Sargent, E. D. (1986). "American Tragedy: Blacks Killing Blacks," Wilmington, DE: *Sunday News Journal,* pp. C1-C4.

Schaskolsky, L. (1970). "The Innocent Bystander and Crime." *Federal Probation* 34:44–48.

Schultz, L. G. (1960). "Why the Negro Carries Weapons." *Journal of Criminal Law, Crime and Police Science* 53:476–83.

Schwartz, F. (1963). "Men's Clothing and the Negro." *Phylon* 124:224–31.

Scully, D. (1990). *Understanding Sexual Violence—A Study of Convicted Rapists*. Boston: Unwin Hyman.

Schlly, D., and J. Marolla (1984). "Convicted Rapists' Vocabulary of Motive: Excuses and Justifications." *Social Problems* 31:530–44.

Secretary's Task Force on Black and Minority Health (1986). *Homicide, Suicide and Unintentional Injuries*. Washington, DC: U.S. Department of Health and Human Services.

Sessions, W. B. (1992). *Crime in the United States*. Washington, DC: U.S. Department of Justice.

Shaw, C., and H. McKay (1942). *Juvenile Delinquency and Urban Areas*. Chicago: University of Chicago Press.

Short, J. F. (1968). "Comment on Lerman's Gangs, Networks and Subcultural Delinquency." *American Journal of Sociology* 73:513–15.

Silberman, C. E. (1978). *Criminal Violence, Criminal Justice*. New York: Random House.

Silverman, I. J., and S. Dinitz (1974). "Compulsive Masculinity and Delinquency: An Empirical Investigation." *Criminology* 11:498–515.

Spivak, H., et al. (1989). "Practitioner Forum: Public Health and the Primary Prevention of Adolescent Violence—The Violence Prevention Project." *Violence and Victims* 4:203–12.

Staples, R. (1974). "Violence and Black America: The Political Implications." *Black World* 23:16–34.

——— (1975). "White Racism, Black Crime and American Justice: An Application of the Colonial Model to Explain Crime and Race." *Phylon* 36:14–22.

——— (1982). *Black Masculinity: The Black Male's Role in American Society*. San Francisco: Black Scholar Press.

——— (1984). "American Racism and High Crime Rates: The Inextricable Connection." *Western Journal of Black Studies* 8:62–71.

Sterne, M. W. (1976). "Drinking Patterns and Alcoholism Among American Negroes," in D. J. Pittman (ed.), *Alcoholism*. New York: Harper and Row, pp. 66–98.

Sterne, M. W., and D. J. Pittman (1972). *Drinking Patterns in the Ghetto*. St. Louis, MO: Social Science Institute, Washington University.

Stokes, R., and J. P. Hewitt (1976). "Aligning Actions." *American Sociological Review* 4:838–49.

Suttles, G. D. (1968). *The Social Order of the Slums*. Chicago: University of Chicago Press.

Sykes, G. M., and D. Matza (1957). "Techniques of Neutralization: A Theory of Delinquency." *American Sociological Review* 22:664–70.

Tardiff, K., et al. (1986). "A Study of Homicides in Manhattan, 1981." *American Journal of Public Health* 76:139–43.

Tift, S. (1990). "Fighting the Failure Syndrome." *Time*, March 21, pp. 83–84.

Toby, J. (1966). "Violence and the Masculine Ideal: Some Qualitative Data." *Annals of the American Academy of Political and Social Science* 364:19–27.

Toch, H. (1969). *Violent Men*. Chicago: Aldine.

——— (1975). *Men in Crisis: Human Breakdowns in Prison*. Chicago: Aldine.

——— (1977). *Living in Prison: The Ecology of Survival*. New York: Free Press.

——— (1980a). "Evolving a Science of Violence." *American Behavioral Scientist* 23:653–665.

——— (1980b). "Toward an Interdisciplinary Approach to Criminal Violence." *Journal of Criminal Law and Criminology* 71:646–53.

——— (1983). "The Catalytic Situation in the Violence Equation." *Journal of Applied Social Psychology* 15:105–23.

Toch, H. (1986). "True to You, Darling, in my Fashion: The Notion of Contingent Consistency," in A. Campbell and J. J. Gibbs (eds.), *Violent Transactions.* New York: Basil Blackwell.

U.S. Bureau of the Census (1983). *America's Black Population 1978–1982.* Washington, DC: Government Printing Office.

U.S. Department of Health (1992). *Health in the United States—1992.* Washington, D.C.: Government Printing Office.

U.S. Department of Health, Education and Welfare (1979). *Health Status of Minorities and Low-Income Groups.* Washington, DC: Government Printing Office.

U.S. Department of Justice (1982). *Criminal Victimization in the United States, 1982.* Washington, DC: Government Printing Office.

U.S. News & World Report (1986). "A Nation Apart." March 17:18–28.

Vontress, C. E. (1971). "The Black Male Personality." *Black Scholar* 2:10–16.

Voss, H., and J. R. Hepburn (1968). "Patterns of Criminal Homicide in Chicago." *Journal of Criminal Law, Criminology and Police Science* 59:499–508.

Wilbanks, W. (1984). *Murder in Miami.* Lantham, MD: University Press of America.

Williams K. (1984). "Economic Sources of Homicide: Restructuring the Effects of Poverty and Inequality." *American Sociological Review* 49:283–89.

Wilson, J. Q., and R. J. Hernstein (1985). *Crime and Human Nature.* New York: Simon and Schuster.

Wilson, W. J. (1990). "Public Policy Research and the Truly Disadvantaged," in C. Jencks and P. E. Peterson (eds.), *The Urban Underclass.* Washington, DC: Brookings Institution.

Wilson, W. J., and K. Neckerman (1987). "Poverty and Family Structure—The Widening Gap Between Evidence and Public Policy Issues," in W. J. Wilson, *The Truly Disadvantaged: The Inner City, the Underclass, and Public Policy.* Chicago: University of Chicago Press, pp. 63–85.

Wilson-Brewer, R., and B. Jacklin (1990). "Violence Prevention Strategies Targeted at the General Population of Minority Youth." Paper presented for the Forum on Youth Violence in Minority Communities: Setting the Agenda for Prevention. Atlanta, GA, December 10–12.

Wolfgang, M. E. (1958). *Patterns of Criminal Homicide.* Philadelphia: University of Pennsylvania Press.

——— (1983). Delinquency in Two Birth Cohorts. *American Behavior Scientist* 27:75–86.

Wolfgang, M. E., et al. (1985). *The National Survey of Crime Severity.* Washington, DC: U.S. Department of Justice.

Wolfgang, M. E., and F. Ferracuti (1967). *The Subculture of Violence.* London: Tavistock.

Zahn, M., and M. Bencivengo (1974). "Violent Death: A Comparison Between Drug Users and Nondrug Users." *Addictive Diseases: An International Journal* 1:282–96.

Zahn, M., and G. Snodgrass (1978). "Drug Use and the Structure of Homicide in Two U.S. Cities," in E. Flynn and J. Conrad (eds.), *The New and the Old Criminology.* New York: Praeger Publishers, pp. 134–50.

Index

Academic failure, effects of, 39
Accounts, violent confrontation/
    process and unacceptable,
    93–98
Age of patron, barroom violence and,
    36
Alcohol
    decision to use violence and use of,
    110–12
    violence and role of, 15–16,
    74–78
Alignment, use of the term, 93–94
"American Tragedy: Blacks Killing
    Blacks" (Sargent), 2
Anderson, E., 25
Anticipation of violence, post-incident
    routine activity, 124–26
Appeal to higher loyalties, 152–53
Athens, L. H., 45, 155
Autonomy norm, 33–34
Autonomy transgressions, 149–50
Avoid trouble rule, 63–64

Bar-hopping image, 31–32
Barroom violence
    age of patron and, 36
    characteristics of bars, 35
    social class and, 36
    studies on, 35–37
Bars
    definition and use of the term, 5, 20
    masculine expression in, 22–34
    significance of, 20

social functions of lower-class,
    20–22
Bar settings, definition and use of the
    term, 5
Bencivengo, M., 17
Berkowitz, L., 155
Black, D., 152
Blumer, H., 4
Brownfield, D., 15
Bureau of Justice Statistics, 2, 16, 17

Campbell, A., 36
Cavan, S., 20
Challenger Boys Club, 162–63
Chicano men, 150
Clark, K. B., 50
Closure of conflict
    internal, 121–22
    overt, 120–21
    resistance to, 122–23
    symbolic, 119–20
Cohen, L. E., 38, 39
Communication, violence as, 112–13
Community-based coalitions, 160
Community centers, multicomponent,
    162–63
Community policing, 163
Compulsive masculinity, definition of,
    50
Compulsive masculinity concept
    as an alternative to traditional mas-
    culinity, 13, 37
    description of, 11–13

191

About the Author

William Oliver has devoted his career to examining the causes and prevention of black on black violence. He is the author of several articles that have been published in academic journals, including the *Journal of Black Studies*, the *Western Journal of Black Studies*, and *Violence & Victims*.

Oliver is a member of the Board of Directors of the National Council of African American Men (NCAM), a national men's group designed to help shape public policy and legislation affecting black males, and is associate editor of the *Journal of African American Studies* (*JAAMS*). A significant highlight of his career involved presenting testimony before a subcommittee of the U.S. Congress on the need for an Afrocentric perspective and correctional education.

Born in upstate New York, Oliver is a graduate of Tuskegge University and the State University of New York at Albany, where he received his Ph.D. in Criminal Justice. He is currently an assistant professor of Criminal Justice at Indiana University, Bloomington.